Hunter's Stew
and Hangtown Fry

ALSO BY LILA PERL
WITH DRAWINGS BY RICHARD CUFFARI

Slumps, Grunts, and Snickerdoodles
What Colonial America Ate and Why

✧

Hunter's Stew
and Hangtown Fry

*What Pioneer America
Ate and Why*

Lila Perl

Pictures by Richard Cuffari

A Clarion Book · The Seabury Press · New York

01,0186

The Seabury Press, 815 Second Avenue, New York, New York 10017

Library of Congress Cataloging in Publication Data

Perl, Lila.
Hunter's stew and hangtown fry, what pioneer America ate and why.
"A Clarion book."   Includes index.
Summary: Examines the diet of nineteenth-century pioneers and the
culinary innovations brought about by the hard life in the Western
territories.
1. Food supply — United States — History — Juvenile literature.
2. Diet — United States — History — Juvenile literature. 3. Cookery,
American — The West — History — Juvenile literature. [1. Food
supply — History. 2. Cookery, American — The West — History]
I. Cuffari, Richard, 1925–   II. Title.
TX360.U6P47   641'.0978   77-5366
ISBN 0-8164-3200-7

✥❧✥

_____

Acknowledgments

Quotations used in the text are from the following:

Bidwell, John. *Echoes of the Past: An Account of the First Emigrant Train to California.* N.Y.: Citadel Press edition, 1962.

Bossidy, John Collins. *Toast to Boston, Midwinter Dinner, Holy Cross Alumni,* 1910.

Bothwick, J. D. *Three Years in California.* Edinburgh and London: William Blackwood & Sons, 1858.

Buffum, Edward Gould. *Six Months in the Gold Fields.* 1850.

de Montezlun, Baron. *Voyage Fait dans les Années 1816 et 1817, de New-Yorck à la Nouvelle-Orléans.* Paris, 1818.

de Tocqueville, Alexis. *Journey to America.* N.Y.: Anchor Books edition, 1971.

Dickens, Charles. *American Notes.* Penguin edition, 1972.

Gleig, George Robert. *A Narrative of the Campaigns of the British Army, at Washington, Baltimore, and New Orleans.* 1814 and 1815.

Humphrey, Seth K. *Following the Prairie Frontier.* Minneapolis: University of Minnesota Press, 1931.

Michaux, François André. *Voyage à l'Ouest des Monts Alléghanys.* Paris, 1804; English translation, 1805.

Parkman, Francis. *The Oregon Trail.* 1847.

Raeder, Ole Munch. *America in the Forties: The Letters of Ole Munch Raeder.* Translated and edited by Gunnar J. Malmin. Minneapolis: University of Minnesota Press, 1929.

Trollope, Mrs. Frances M. *Domestic Manners of the Americans.* London, 1832.

Twain, Mark. *A Tramp Abroad.* N.Y.: Harper & Brothers, 1879, 1899, 1907.

von Hübner, Joseph Alexander, Baron. *Promenade Autour du Monde, 1871.* Paris, 1873; English translation, London, 1874.

Contents

✅ RECIPES

The Century
of Pioneer America

PIONEER AMERICA CONJURES UP images of the Kentucky frontiersman in his coonskin cap, of the Nebraska sodbuster, of wagon trains rolling west across the Rockies to the Pacific. Scouts and trappers, farmers and traders, gold miners and railroad builders were all wilderness pioneers during the hundred years or so following the Revolutionary War, years that witnessed the astonishing expansion and development of the young United States.

During the nineteenth century the nation grew from a group of former colonies perched on the eastern seaboard of North America to a broad continent bounded by mighty oceans. But those who tamed the wild land — sometimes well and sometimes carelessly — were not the only pioneers of that era. Newcomers to established towns and cities faced a similar challenge in shaping an expanding America.

They were pioneers of another kind; construction crews and coal miners, mill workers and factory hands, garment makers and shopkeepers. Their lives were less threatened perhaps by the hazards of nature but were no less demanding or exhausting. For the pioneers of the cities had to break new ground in a fast-growing and

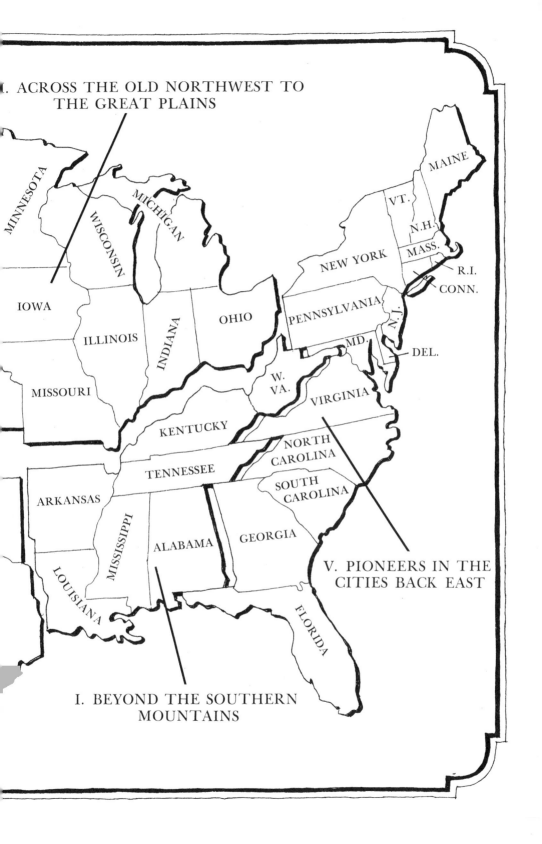

II. ACROSS THE OLD NORTHWEST TO
THE GREAT PLAINS

MINNESOTA

MICHIGAN

WISCONSIN

MAINE

VT.

N.H.

NEW YORK

MASS.

R.I.

CONN.

IOWA

ILLINOIS

INDIANA

OHIO

PENNSYLVANIA

N.J.

MD.

DEL.

MISSOURI

W. VA.

VIRGINIA

KENTUCKY

NORTH CAROLINA

TENNESSEE

ARKANSAS

SOUTH CAROLINA

MISSISSIPPI

ALABAMA

GEORGIA

V. PIONEERS IN THE
CITIES BACK EAST

LOUISIANA

FLORIDA

I. BEYOND THE SOUTHERN
MOUNTAINS

usually alien society, thousands of miles from their homelands.

Between 1800 and 1900 the population of the United States soared from 5 million to 75 million. There were over 20 million new arrivals, not only from England, Africa, Scotland, Ireland, the Netherlands, Germany, and Scandinavia, as during the colonial period, but also from Italy, France, Switzerland, Austria, Russia, Poland, Portugal, Greece, Turkey, China, and Canada.

Except for the African slaves, who did not come of their own volition, journeying to the New World was undertaken for a number of reasons — religious liberty, escape from wars and unrest, economic enterprise, adventure, even curiosity. Not the least of these motives was hunger or freedom from the fear of recurrent food shortages. Some came to America in pursuit of a better diet or even of a rare and valuable foodstuff, as in the case of Columbus, who came, mistakenly, in search of the spices of the East Indies.

By the 1700s, the thirteen colonies were bolstered in their conviction to wrench free of Britain largely by America's self-sufficiency in food. America's surpluses of grain, pork, beef, and fish were already being traded abroad for molasses, sugar, spices, dried fruits, tea, coffee, and wines. And all through the pioneering 1800s, letters flowed back across the Atlantic urging relatives and friends from the devastated potato fields of Ireland to the despairing villages of Russia to come to the land where bread was plentiful, meat was eaten three times a day, and pie for breakfast was commonplace.

We can read the history of the nineteenth century United States in terms of its politics and legislation, its economic development, its military campaigns, its treatment of the Indian population, the massive issue of slavery. We can also trace that century as social history, examining the ways in which Americans lived and worked and how they evolved from the pinched, hardy race of the post-Revolution frontier to the showy citizens of the Gilded Age, those decades toward the close of the century when many Americans were overfed, overdressed, wealthy and powerful beyond the dreams of the early pioneers.

The foods people eat, their cooking and dining customs and their changing culinary patterns tell us a great deal about their broader social history. Pioneer America, with wave upon wave of newly arrived ethnic groups, was a time and a place of rich cultural ferment. And often the cooking pot was both an expression and a reflection of the larger social scene.

A campfire cauldron of freshly shot meat simmering into a hunter's stew, an inflation-tagged Hangtown fry gobbled up in a California gold-rush eatery, the extravagant wedding breakfasts and dinner parties given by the rich and the super-rich — each tells us something illuminating and evocative about the century of pioneer America.

Beyond the Southern Mountains

"THE RESIDENTS OF KENTUCKY EA-gerly recommend their state to strangers as the best part of the United States. There the soil is most fertile, the climate most salubrious, and all the inhabitants are there because they were attracted by the love of liberty and independence!" These words were written by a traveler from France, François André Michaux, who in 1802 ventured west of the Appalachians into the rough frontiering country beyond the southern mountains.

For hundreds of years colonial America had nestled between the Atlantic Ocean on the east and the lofty horizons of the Alleghenies, the Blue Ridge, and the Great Smokies, on the west. All were ranges of the majestic land barrier known as the Appalachian Mountains.

Early explorers who had climbed their thickly forested and well-watered southerly heights, which were almost always enveloped in a misty blue haze, actually believed that they saw a great sea shimmering in the distance. At the Appalachians, they said, the continent ended and beyond lay an expanse of water upon which one could set sail for China.

Daniel Boone and other scouts and hunters of the mid-1700s were to prove that this was not so. The only sea that lay beyond the mountains of western Virginia and North Carolina was a sea of game. For here was a land much richer than the coastal South with its sandy lowlands, swamps, and marshes. In the lush Kentucky country, deer, elk, and black bear were abundant, while squirrel, rabbit, raccoon, quail, grouse, and other small game were simply taken for granted. The wild turkeys were so immensely fat that they often went crashing to the ground when they attempted to roost in the limbs of the trees. Well-worn buffalo tracks leading to salt licks made ideal foot trails for the Indians and for the first "long hunters," as the frontier scouts with their long-barreled, muzzle-loading rifles were called.

With so much game waiting to be brought down, it was not surprising that the Indians of the Kentucky-West Virginia-Tennessee region did only a moderate amount of planting. They were mainly Shawnees, of the Algonquian family, and Cherokees, a southern branch of the Iroquois. Here corn was the Indians' agricultural mainstay. It was either ground into meal for cornbread or porridge, or eaten as hominy, whole corn kernels with the hulls removed.

The Indians had devised a means of producing lye from wood ashes and then cooking the dried corn kernels in lye water to make the hard, coarse coverings slip off easily. As lye is a dangerous poison, the hominy had to undergo numerous washings before it was safe to eat. Hominy hearts stewed with chunks of meat or simply boiled in water and served with bear grease made a pleasant change from a diet of meat, meat, meat. Beans, pumpkins, squash, melons, and sweet potatoes were cultivated, too. But the Indian hominy (the name comes from the Algonquian word, *rockahominie*) seemed destined to become a special favorite among the Southern settlers. While whole hearts are sometimes called "big hominy," the coarsely ground kernels are known as "small hominy," or grits. To this day, grits, prepared from white rather than yellow corn, make a favorite Southern breakfast served with flavorful country-smoked ham and fried eggs.

Hickory nuts, walnuts, blackberries, and persimmons made good wild pickings for the Indian dwellers of the Kentucky country. The persimmon is a small scarlet fruit that tastes almost as puckery as it sounds unless it is permitted to ripen on the tree until frost. The pioneers of Tennessee later became famous for their persimmon breads and puddings baked with the sweetly ripe and mellow pulp of this native fruit.

"Liberty and independence," despite the words of François Michaux, were not really the main attractions that drew the first frontiersmen to Kentucky. Boone, it is true, appeared to love the challenge of the wilderness and considered neighbors closer than forty miles away a threat to his independence. But the real lure of the land beyond the mountains was the promise of rich hunting for animal skins and furs. Europe could not get enough of the deer leathers, huge warm buffalo pelts, deep thick bearskins, and smaller furs for trimmings and piecings that came from the New World. Wild mink was especially prized, while raccoon skins were so common that Europeans believed all Americans wore coonskin caps. Benjamin Franklin helped to establish this impression when, as minister to France, he appeared in Paris in 1777 in a coonskin cap complete with tail.

Despite the hardships of hunting and trapping in a wilderness of almost impassable mountains, dense tangled forests, and thickly matted meadowlands, the settlers were never far behind the lone frontiersmen.

Scout, Indian trader, fur trapper, lumberman, farmer—all were links in the pattern of pioneering, one following on the heels of the other.

Beginning in 1788, a great migration of farmers from Virginia, North Carolina, Pennsylvania, and other easterly points took to the Wilderness Road, a trail that began in Virginia and inched through the Cumberland Gap, a natural pass in the Appalachians that led into Kentucky. The road was narrow, rough, and winding, pocked with tree stumps, pitted with deep holes, often blocked by fallen trees. Understandably, the Indians of the region added to the pioneers' hardships by resisting the encroachment. Most of these Indians would later be pushed westward all the way to Oklahoma.

The settlers were mainly of English, Scottish, Irish, and German stock. By 1792, Kentucky was so well populated that it became the first "western" state to be admitted to the Union. It was the second to achieve statehood after the Revolution, Vermont preceding it in 1791.

꿍

Pot Luck on the Kentucky Frontier

THE FIRST SHELTERS OF THE KENTUCKY pioneers were crude log houses hastily built in a clearing. The chinks between the raw logs were usually filled in with mud, but often it cracked and fell out or washed away in a driving rain. In a visit to America in 1831, the

famous French traveler and observer, Alexis de Tocqueville, speaks of reaching a Kentucky farm cabin "through whose walls a fire can be seen crackling on the hearth." De Tocqueville concludes that, in these houses, "one is scarcely better protected than one would be in a shelter made of leafy branches."

The pioneers had numerous other problems as well. The supplies of cornmeal, wheat flour, and salt that they brought with them on the Wilderness Road soon gave out. Waiting for the first corn crop, planted haphazardly among the stumps of newly felled trees, was often a dismal time. Starvation was not a threat, for game was everywhere. But a steady diet of meat made the settlers long for a bit of bread. Roasted breast of wild turkey came to be known jokingly as "hunter's bread." It was dry and grainy, and provided some contrast to the red meat that steadily found its way into the stewpot. A "hunter's stew" could contain anything from chunks of bear meat to bits of squirrel meat. One common requirement was strong red pepper to mask the gamey flavor of some of the meat that got tossed into the kettle.

Salt was another scarce item on the Kentucky frontier until the settlers began to organize annual trips to the salt deposits frequented by the roaming deer and buffalo of the region. The pioneers would try to bring back enough salt to last a year for preserving meats and making vegetables and starchy foods more palatable. Sugar and other sweeteners were scarce, too. In the early days, settlers collected wild honey, and some were lucky enough to find stands of sugar maples nearby. Like the colonists of the Northeast, they drew the sap and boiled it down into maple syrup.

Wheat did poorly in the too-rich Kentucky soil and was difficult to harvest in the patchwork, stump-ridden fields. But peas, beans, turnips, cabbages, potatoes, and all the Indian crops of the squash family did well. With the coming of spring, everybody went out in search of "garden sass," wild greens that could be chewed on fresh for their succulent leafy tenderness or cooked for flavor with a bit of hog jowl, bacon, or other cured meat. A "mess o' greens" made a pleasant change from the dried and root vegetables that the pioneer family had been living on all winter. But one had to be careful gathering greens to eat in a new territory. Some varieties were poisonous, especially after the first shoots appeared and the plants, really weeds, began to mature.

"Hogs are the most numerous of the domestic animals; they are kept by all the inhabitants." So wrote Michaux in 1802, and indeed these half-wild pigs, their ears notched so their owners could identify them, foraged merrily in the woods and were fed corn besides. Autumn, however, brought the day of reckoning for the full-grown animals, for this was hog-killing time. It was a family and often a community event since the entire animal had to be used. Hams, shoulders, and sides of bacon were salted and smoked for future use; trimmings were chopped fine and made into sausage; fat was rendered into lard; and spareribs and internal organs were usually eaten fresh. Cracklings, the crisp brown bits and pieces left over from lard-rendering, went into cracklin' bread. They made a flavorful addition to the almost unvarying cornbread of the frontier.

The pioneers kept dairy and beef cattle, too, but in smaller quantities than hogs. Beef was best preserved by salting, and in Kentucky (unlike New England where salt was more plentiful and salt beef very popular) the salt was often more costly than the beef. Or perhaps the settlers simply preferred pork.

Tennesseans became famous for their "ham 'n redeye gravy." This was salty, home-smoked ham, so well aged it had a greenish mold on the outside that had to be scraped off, so hard it had to be soaked overnight and simmered in water for hours before it was ready to be sliced for frying. But, of course, such ham, unlike the pink, watery, packing-house hams of today, had real "down home" flavor. The red-eye gravy came from mixing the frying-pan drippings with black coffee and a little water. It was called red-eye because the black coffee in the gravy was supposed to keep you awake all night—along, no doubt, with a terrible thirst! Bland accompaniments like grits and hot fluffy biscuits plus a mess of cooked greens were just right for Tennessee ham with red-eye gravy.

The abundance of corn grown on the Kentucky frontier soon led to the home manufacture of corn whiskey. The mountain barrier of the Applachians had cut off the coastal supply of rum, and the rigors of pioneer life seemed to demand a strong alcoholic beverage as an eye-opener at breakfast time, as insulation against the cold, as an anesthetic against pain, and as an antiseptic for snakebites and other wounds. "Corn likker," harsh and throat-searing, was distilled in almost every frontier cabin. Later, its manufacture was improved, and it became known as bourbon whiskey because so much of it was originally made in Bourbon County, Kentucky.

The lonely lives of the frontier families were relieved from time to time by communal activities that combined work with recreation. Pioneer Americans of the energetic young United States seemed so accustomed to performing endless chores that very likely they would have felt awkward and even guilty at idle play. Special occasions and the seasons themselves brought their own events. Spring might mean a barn-raising, autumn a cornhusking bee. Neighbors gathered so that many hands might make light work. At the same time, everyone indulged eagerly in the social atmosphere, trading gossip, dancing to the tunes of local fiddlers, eyeing potential marriage partners. Husking bees were especially popular with young people. The mountain of unshucked ears of corn was divided in two and the side that finished stripping the ears first won. Better still, a youth who found an ear with red kernels on it had the right to command a kiss from any girl he chose (and girls who found red ears probably had them smuggled, along with embarrassed giggles, into the hands of the boys they hoped would ask a kiss of them).

Food and drink were important adjuncts to the pioneer get-together, whether it was a gruff, hearty outdoor event like a wood-sawing contest or a fireside quilting bee for women and girls only. At large public gatherings, one of the most popular dishes was Kentucky burgoo. Originally burgoo was the name for a British seaman's thick oatmeal porridge. Somehow, in Kentucky, it became transformed into a rich and somewhat refined version of a hunter's stew.

Some burgoo recipes call for squirrel and chicken, but rabbit, beef, pork, and veal can also be used. Vegetables, too, are included—corn, lima beans, onions, and potatoes, and often tomatoes, celery, cabbage, carrots, peppers, turnips, and almost anything else available. Like hunter's stew, a burgoo should be peppery, but it should also be quite thick and is sometimes cooked almost to a heavy mash.

As the century advanced, a political rally, a church supper, a horse sale or horseracing event became the perfect occasion for enlisting the talents of a crew of burgoo chefs, and the occasion itself would be known as a "burgoo." The food would be cooked outdoors in huge iron kettles for nearly an entire day. Then the hot stew would be dished up to the crowd in tin cups.

Burgoo recipes exist for making 1200 gallons! At campaign rallies in particular, beer, whiskey, and other drinks would be provided to help put out the fire of the burgoo's rich, peppery flavor, and many a local politician was probably elected to office on the strength of the "burgoo" to which the neighborhood farmers and townsmen were invited.

If the promise of the land beyond the Appalachians was great, that of the land *beyond* the beyond was even greater. Almost everyone seemed imbued with the idea of making successive moves westward. To remain in one place was not only to stand still; it was considered almost the equivalent of moving backward. Only the Pennsylvania Germans of southeastern Pennsylvania, who had arrived in the late 1600s and were popularly known as the "Pennsylvania Dutch," seemed immune to the westering impulses of so many farm families in the years following the Revolution. Perhaps it was the strong religious dictates of their Christian sects—Amish, Mennonite, Dunkard—that held them together in their original place of settlement, farming intensively but husbanding the land with care, just as they had done in crowded, land-hungry Europe.

For the average American of the early 1800s, the sense of living on the edge of a great continent of untold potential was overpowering. The Kentucky pioneers were no exception and many saw the fifteenth state of the Union as a mere stopping place before moving on to greener pastures. A family's one- or two-room cabin and partially-improved patch of farmland offering good timbering and hunting could easily be sold for hard cash to the next wave of easterners heading west. The more adventurous went on to break new ground in what would again probably be only a temporary place of habitation. If there was a measure of wastefulness, an

The cuisine was one of mouth-watering plenty. It utilized the wild and cultivated foods of the warm southland as well as many rich, imported delicacies brought upriver from New Orleans. Most of all, its dishes required time, skill, and ample labor for preparation.

Indian corn, for example, was made into rich, delicate dishes like hominy pudding and corn custard into which the cook ladled milk, cream, eggs, and butter with a generous hand. In the South, with its long growing season, corn pudding was prepared with fresh, sweet kernels stripped from newly-picked young ears. It was then served as one of the many accompaniments gracing the main course.

A pre-Civil War dinner menu on a Mississippi Valley cotton plantation might well have included oysters, turtle soup, baked ham, fried chicken with cream gravy, corn pudding, sweet potato pone, hot biscuits, baked squash, cooked garden vegetables, jellies, dessert puddings, and several kinds of pies, including peach, sweet potato, and pecan.

The nation's great nineteenth-century pie-eating binge is believed to have originated in the South, largely as a result of sugar becoming more plentiful. Not only was this important sweetener imported directly from the West Indies through New Orleans, but canefields had also been developed in Louisiana around 1750, and sugar refineries had soon been built along the Mississippi. Colonial New England had long depended on shipments of molasses from the Caribbean for sweetening its pie fillings, but the use of that cheaper sweetener, a by-product of sugar refining, now passed into decline.

Southern pie fillings ran the gamut of fruits, vegetables, custards, and nut mixtures. In Mississippi, pecans native to the region were combined with eggs, butter, sugar, and corn syrup, to make one of the sweetest, most gooey, and yet toothsome pies ever created—pecan pie.

Also truly Southern in character is the fried pie. Alabama often takes credit for this dessert although it is found in virtually every part of the South. To prepare a fried pie, the pastry is rolled out into a small round. A mound of a well-thickened filling is placed in the center, the pastry is flipped over to make a half moon, the edges are sealed, and the pie is fried quickly in a kettle of deep fat. Among the favorite fillings are peaches, apples, and wild blackberry jam. The hot golden-brown pies are dusted with a snow of powdered sugar and eaten warm.

As sugar became steadily cheaper, the variety of pies baked in the slave-staffed Southern kitchens became part of the American cuisine. Other regions of the country contributed their own fruit and berry fillings, and pie-eating, even at breakfast, began to sweep the nation.

⋙⋘

The Creole Cookery
of Louisiana

NEW ORLEANS WAS THE HUB OF THAT exotic new world that appeared so threatening to some of the staid New Englanders who opposed the Louisiana Purchase. Its population included French and Spanish people, whose intermarriage had created a mixture of the two cultures known as Creole. Also living there were black African slaves brought from the West Indies as well as directly from Africa, many slave and free peoples of mixed African and Creole blood, and Canadian French, who had migrated south after the British began to gain control of Canada in the mid-1700s. These last were known as "Cajuns," a slurring of the word Acadians, as most of the newcomers were from the easternmost provinces of Canada, then popularly known as Acadia.

Upon his arrival in New Orleans on New Year's Day of 1832, Alexis de Tocqueville noted the "forest of ships" on the Mississippi, the contrast of lowly huts and unpaved, muddy streets with the numerous fine houses of the city—flat-roofed Spanish dwellings with lacy irongrillwork balconies, French mansions with broad carriage entrances, and stately English homes constructed of brick. "Population just as mixed," de Tocqueville jotted in his notebook. "Faces with every shade of color. Language French, English, Spanish, Creole." He felt, he said, as though he were "a thousand leagues from the United States."

A bewildering mixture, too, was the cookery of this highly flavored city. In addition to the Creole, a strong culinary influence was traceable to the Indians of the region. Most of the lower Mississippi Valley had been inhabited by the Natchez people and by Choctaws, Chickasaws, and Creeks of the Muskhogean family. The Choctaw Indians of Louisiana had developed a thickening agent for stews and soups, known as filé powder. This substance, made from the dried, pulverized leaves of the sassafras plant, had been used chiefly for medicinal purposes by the Indians. The (mainly black) Creole cooks of New Orleans, however, took filé a step further, incorporating it with seafood, onions, green peppers, and tomatoes into a hot stew known as gumbo.

The name gumbo owes its origins neither to the Spanish-French nor to the Indians, but to the black inhabitants of Louisiana. The word has two other applications besides: the French dialect spoken by the Louisiana slaves was called Gumbo; and okra, a podlike African vegetable introduced by the black slaves, was also called gumbo.

In preparing a Louisiana shrimp, crab, or all-vegetable gumbo, it is customary to add either the filé powder of the Choctaws or the okra of the Africans. The latter has a mucilaginous quality, so it too acts as a thickener. New Orleans people lean to filé; other Louisianians to okra. It is not really necessary or correct to use both in a gumbo. The dish should be fairly soupy, in any case, and it is usually served in a deep plate or bowl over a bed of hot, fluffy white rice.

Rice had been grown throughout much of the American South from colonial times. Louisiana grew so much that, by the early 1700s, it was exporting part of its crop. Rice predominates in a New Orleans dish called jambalaya, a mixture containing ham, chicken, shrimp, sausage, and even oysters, as well as Creole vegetables—onions, green peppers, and tomatoes. This popular vegetable combination also crops up in shrimp Creole, red snapper Creole, and along with other succulent catches from the Mississippi and the Gulf of Mexico.

The tomato, a key Creole ingredient, had led a shadowy life in the United States until it was introduced into the cuisine via New Orleans. Although a native food of Central and South America, Europeans believed the tomato to be poisonous, and between the early 1500s and the early 1800s it was cultivated in Europe and parts of North America as an ornamental plant, prized for its handsome scarlet "love apples." After the tomato was reinstated in the New World as an acceptable food, cooks in the United States began to make the most of it. Patent medicine salesmen traveled around the country selling tomato "tonics" and "compound of tomato" pills as early as 1825, and later in the century the tomato became the main ingredient of ketchup, the "national sauce" to be dumped on everything and anything.

New Orleans was a gateway for other foods rarely eaten elsewhere in North America. Not long after the French founded the city, in 1718, France sent shiploads of young women to the New World to provide wives for the early settlers. Known as "casket girls" because the French government provided each girl with a casket or chest of dowry articles, the new arrivals found themselves quite unprepared for some of the foods of America. Their chief complaint was the impossibility of baking the long, delicate, crisp-crusted bread of France with an ingredient as coarse and tasteless as cornmeal. The young brides demanded the fine white wheat flour of France so that they could also reproduce the favorite rolls of their homeland, flaky, crescent-shaped *croissants,* rich, buttery *brioches,* and round, puffy French doughnuts known as *beignets soufflés,* so light they were often compared to a "nun's sigh." They and their descendants were so rigid in their refusal to compromise with cornmeal that the wheat flour was imported until wheat was grown in greater quantity in the New World.

As bread of precious wheat flour was not to be wasted even when it became stale, the thrifty French wives soaked it in a sweetened mixture of milk and eggs, fried

it in butter, and served it with honey or preserves. They called this dish *pain perdu* ("lost bread"), but it has come to be known all over the United States as French toast. In view of this being such a tasty rejuvenation of old bread, one wonders why the French did not elect to call it *pain trouvé,* or "found bread."

Cornmeal never took hold in the New Orleans cuisine, but rice found its way into fritters, light golden-brown fried cakes delicately flavored with lemon or vanilla. These were called *calas,* and it became a tradition for the freshly prepared delicacies to be sold on Sunday mornings after church in the old French Quarter of New Orleans. *"Belles calas, tout chaud!"* the black women vendors would call out. "Beautiful calas, nice and hot!" The calas would be taken home to be enjoyed at a late breakfast with large cups of French *café au lait,* half coffee, half hot milk.

After a sumptuous New Orleans dinner, it was the custom to serve, in the French manner, a demitasse of black coffee or, on very special occasions, *café brûlot* (coffee with burnt brandy). The preparation of this beverage involved pouring hot, strong coffee over a bowl of flaming brandy, sugar, orange rind, lemon rind, cinnamon, and cloves. The room would be darkened for the dramatic moment. As soon as the flames died, the spectacular brew was ladled into small coffee cups and handed round to the guests.

Often, a finishing touch was the offering of pralines. These were velvety, fudgelike, patty-shaped confections composed of brown sugar, butter, and pecan nuts. "Cream" pralines, even richer, contained cream as well. Yet these candies were considered an aid to digestion! Their name is derived from that of a French diplomat, Praslin, whose butler is said to have advised a similar confection prepared with almonds and white sugar as an antidote to the effects of overeating. In their American adaptation, the almonds were exchanged for Louisiana-grown pecans and the white sugar for brown.

᪥᪥᪥

The Slave & Indian Communities of the South

ON THE SURFACE, THE AMERICAN SOUTH seemed headed for prosperous times during the first half of the nineteenth century. The pioneering spirit had served to burst through the Appalachians, open and develop the Kentucky frontier, and to bring a vigorous plantation economy and active trading and commercial life to the Mississippi and Gulf regions.

Appearances, however, were deceptive. Slavery, upon which the economy was built, had lent the South a false sense of security. This was proven by the Civil War and its aftermath. In addition, the South attracted very few of the European immigrants who began arriving in the United States in large numbers after 1830, thus depriving the region of fresh enterprise and vitality. The new arrivals stayed away because the South's plantation economy was already well supplied with slave labor, because towns were few, and opportunities for newcomers were far more limited than in the territory north of the Ohio River.

Among the slave population of the South, living conditions varied but were always far below the standards of the white population. "Through the whole of the low country," François André Michaux tells us, "the agricultural labors are performed by Negroes. The planters even use them to drag the plough; they think the land is thus better cultivated and calculate besides that in the course of a year a horse, for food and care, costs more than a slave whose annual expense does not exceed fifteen dollars." Michaux reported that the slaves lived on corn nine months of the year, "the other three months they are fed upon yams," while "meat they never receive."

The more enlightened slave-holders were only slightly more humane. George Washington's slaves at Mount Vernon were permitted to keep small gardens and a few hens, received twenty salt herrings each month, and a little salted meat at harvest time.

Even worse, because they had no hope of the future, was the plight of the first Americans, the Indians. President Jefferson was of the opinion that the Indians would be best off less scattered about and with their holdings condensed to small parcels of land. De Tocqueville was told by a white settler in 1831, "It is a race that is dying out. They are not made for civilization; it kills them." Angered and discouraged, the young Frenchman concluded, "The Indian races are melting in the presence of European civilization like snow in the rays of the sun."

The very survival of the Southern pioneers had depended on the foods first cultivated by the Indians and on hunting and trapping techniques learned from them, while the expansive cookery of the lower Mississippi Valley and the innovative cuisine of New Orleans owed an enormous debt to the talents and labors of the enslaved blacks. The contributions of these two groups, along with those of the early settlers of European origin, can never be clearly separated or carefully weighed. All were pioneers in the land beyond the southern mountains.

Recipes from

Beyond the
Southern Mountains

⋘ BURGOO

    3   tablespoons bacon fat, butter, or margarine
    2   large onions, diced into ¼-inch pieces
    1   pound boneless veal, from shoulder, trimmed
        and cut in 1½-inch chunks (keep any bones)
    1   2½-pound chicken, frying or roasting type,
        washed and cut in eighths
    1   one-pound can stewed tomatoes with liquid *
    2½ teaspoons salt
    ¼   teaspoon black pepper
    ½   teaspoon red (cayenne) pepper
    1   cup celery, washed, trimmed, and cut in one-
        inch chunks
    2   medium-large potatoes, pared and cut in one-
        inch chunks
    2   cups fresh lima beans or one 10-ounce pack-
        age frozen baby lima beans

---

*Or use 4 large fresh tomatoes, skinned and cut in chunks, adding enough water to make 2 cups. To skin tomatoes, place whole tomatoes in deep bowl, cover with boiling water, and let stand 5 minutes. Skins will loosen and peel easily.

1½ cups cooked fresh corn kernels or one 12-
ounce can vacuum-packed kernel corn, well
drained
1 tablespoon flour

Melt 2 tablespoons of the fat in a deep, heavy-bot-
tomed, 4-quart stewpot. Add onions and brown lightly.
Remove with a slotted spoon and set aside. Add remaining tablespoon of fat and heat to sizzling. Add veal
(along with any bones saved from the trimming) and
cook quickly at high heat, stirring with a wooden spoon,
until meat loses its pink color.

Add chicken, tomatoes, salt, black and red pepper,
and celery. Return onions to pot, cover it tightly, reduce
heat to low, and simmer about one hour or until chicken
is tender.

Remove chicken and add potatoes and lima beans to
stewpot. Cover and simmer about one-half hour or until
vegetables are done. After chicken has cooled slightly,
remove meat in large chunks, discarding skin and
bones. Return chicken to stewpot when potatoes and
lima beans are tender. Add corn.

To thicken stew liquid, put one tablespoon of flour
into a small bowl. Add 2 tablespoons cold water and beat
with fork or wire whisk until perfectly smooth. Add 6 tablespoons of hot stew liquid, blend well, return mixture
to stewpot and simmer stew gently a few minutes until
liquid becomes thickened. Check flavor, adding additional seasoning if necessary.

Burgoo is just right served with a tart, vinegary salad
of wilted greens or cabbage slaw and with hot cornbread
or corn sticks. It can be made a day ahead and tastes
even better when reheated. Serves 6-8.

⋖ *CORN PUDDING*

  2   eggs, large
1½ cups fresh cooked corn or one 12-ounce can
      vacuum-packed whole kernel corn, drained
      of any liquid
  3   tablespoons flour
  ¾ teaspoon salt
  ⅛ teaspoon white pepper
  2   tablespoons melted butter (or margarine)
  1   cup "half-and-half" (or ½ cup milk and ½ cup
      light cream)
  ⅔ cup milk

Preheat oven to 325 degrees Fahrenheit.

In a medium-large mixing bowl, beat eggs with a wire whisk. Add remaining ingredients in order given. Pour mixture into a buttered 1½-quart casserole or baking dish. Place casserole in a pan containing hot water to a depth of about one inch.

Bake pudding one hour or until center is firm when touched gently and a sharp knife inserted into center comes out clean. Serve hot, directly from baking dish. Corn pudding makes a fine accompaniment to crisply fried chicken or roast pork. Makes 6 servings.

⋖ *PECAN PIE*

Pie Crust *

  1   cup sifted all-purpose flour
  ½ teaspoon salt

---

  *If preferred, use a commercial pie-crust mix, making up pastry for one 9-inch pie shell according to directions on package, or use a commercially prepared, unbaked 9-inch pie shell.

2½   tablespoons vegetable shortening or lard
3   tablespoons chilled butter
3   tablespoons cold water

Pie Filling

3   eggs
2   tablespoons flour
⅔   cup dark brown sugar, firmly packed
¾   cup light corn syrup
¼   cup melted butter or margarine (½ stick or ⅛ pound)
1   teaspoon vanilla extract
⅛   teaspoon salt
1¼   cups pecan halves or large broken pieces

To prepare pie crust, combine flour and salt in a medium-large mixing bowl. With a pastry blender, or two knives worked in a crisscross motion, cut in the vegetable shortening (or lard) and butter until texture of the flour-and-fat mixture resembles coarse bread crumbs. Add the water, one tablespoon at a time, stirring with a fork so that moisture is evenly distributed. Mix vigorously until large clumps are formed and, with fingers, gather dough quickly into a ball. Place on floured board or pastry cloth, flatten ball slightly, and roll with a floured rolling pin into a circle about 11 inches in diameter. Fit pastry loosely into a 9-inch pie plate. With floured fingers, form a standing rim of dough and pinch or flute it as desired. Set oven to 425 degrees Fahrenheit and place pie crust in refrigerator while preparing filling.

In a medium-large mixing bowl, beat eggs very well with a wire whisk. Beat in flour. Add brown sugar, corn syrup, melted butter, vanilla, and salt, blending each ingredient in with whisk. Take pie crust from refrigerator, distribute pecan halves on bottom, and pour egg-and-sugar mixture on top.

Bake pie 10 minutes at 425 degrees. Then reduce oven heat to 325 degrees and continue baking pie for 30 to 35 minutes, or until center is firm when lightly pressed with finger. Cool pie in oven, with heat turned off and door slightly ajar. Serve pecan pie at room temperature or chilled, with whipped cream if desired. As this pie is very rich, cut small portions. Serves 8-10.

⋖ *SHRIMP GUMBO*

2	cups shelled, medium-size, raw shrimp, cleaned and washed*
4	tablespoons butter or margarine
1	medium onion, cut in ¼-inch dice
1	medium green pepper, cut in ¼-inch dice
2	cups okra, cut in ¼-inch slices (use fresh okra or a 10-ounce package of frozen okra)
1	one-pound can stewed tomatoes, with liquid
¾	teaspoon salt
⅛	teaspoon red (cayenne) pepper
1	bay leaf

Clean shrimp well, removing black thread running along back, and pat dry. Melt 2 tablespoons of the butter or margarine in a large deep skillet that has a cover. When fat is sizzling, add shrimp and sauté quickly for 2 to 3 minutes, tossing with wooden spoon. Cooking shrimp too long will toughen them. Remove shrimp with a slotted spoon and set aside in a bowl.

Add remaining 2 tablespoons of fat to skillet. Add onion, green pepper, and okra. Cook 5 minutes at medium-high heat. Add tomatoes, seasonings, and bay leaf.

---

*If precleaned, precooked shrimp are used, toss lightly in melted fat just to coat and remove at once. Do not sauté.

Cover skillet and cook 25 minutes at low heat. Add shrimp, heat through gently, and serve.

Gumbo should be served over boiled white rice. To prepare rice, combine 1¼ cups long-grain, raw rice, 2½ cups water, 1½ teaspoons salt, and 2 tablespoons butter in a 2-quart saucepan. Cover pan tightly, bring to boil, reduce heat to very low, and cook about 20 minutes, or until rice is tender and all the water is absorbed. This recipe for shrimp gumbo with rice serves 6.

Across the Old Northwest to the Great Plains

$\sim\!\!\delta\!\!\delta\!\!\sim$

O NCE THE APPALACHIAN MOUN-
tain barrier had been breached, there was no holding back the swelling westerly movement of America's pioneers. Across the Ohio River, to the north and
west, lay that immense region of lakes and rivers, of
woodlands, prairies, and plains that was to become the
great heartland of the United States. This seemingly
endless expanse of frontier was arrested only by the
awesome peaks of the Rockies.

Soon after the close of the Revolutionary War, the
government began offering land grants to its veteran
soldiers as compensation for their services. Along with
some enterprising and intrepid families from Virginia
and the Middle Atlantic states, many of Scotch-Irish
background, these pioneers tackled the difficult passage
across the Alleghenies into the Northwest Territory, as
it was then called.

Later in the century, after the Pacific Northwest had
been explored and settled, the clustered states of Ohio,
Indiana, Illinois, Michigan, Wisconsin, and part of Minnesota (east of the Mississippi River) came to be referred
to as the "Old Northwest."

Here, at the turn of the eighteenth century, lay a

dense wilderness that was bursting with wildlife, its waters jumping with fish. Trees, vines, and bushes hung with wild fruit—crabapples, plums, cherries, persimmons, pawpaws, grapes, and blackberries. French traders of the early 1700s had found most of these fruits unbearably sour and astringent compared to the cultivated varieties of Europe. But the blackberries were large and juicy, and the pawpaw, an oblong bananalike fruit, was acceptable, although often so bland in flavor that it was nearly tasteless. Nuts were abundant and toothsome, and included hickories, butternuts, black walnuts, and dwarf chestnuts called chinquapins that were delicious roasted over an open fire.

All of this natural bounty was enjoyed by the Indians of the Old Northwest, who were mainly of the Algonquian and Siouan families, and included tribal groups of the Chippewa, Illinois, Miami, Sauk, and Shawnee. Although they were corn-growers as well as hunters and gatherers, the Indians of the lake regions also had a natural-growing grain that could be harvested for food. This grain was produced by a tall, seed-bearing grass that was found standing in reedy shallows with its "feet in the water." It came to be known as "wild rice."

On the evergreen-forested shores of Michigan, Wisconsin, and Minnesota that skirted Lake Superior, wild rice was especially plentiful. In September, when the seed was ripe on the seven-foot stalks, the Indians would glide among them in their canoes, simply shaking the ears into their boats. After drying the grain, they trampled it inside skin bags to separate the seeds from the chaff. The seeds were then either pounded into flour or cooked whole in water and flavored with animal fat or with oil pressed from butternuts. As in the case of most wild foods, the supply of wild rice has long been outstripped by the demand. Its cost today is roughly twenty times greater than that of cultivated rice, placing this one-time American Indian grain in a luxury class along with other rare foods of the world such as caviar and truffles.

Fresh water fish from the Great Lakes and the numerous rivers and streams gave the Indians a *sagamité,* or hominy dish, combined with fish and flavored with marrow from the bones of elk or moose. Pike, whitefish, trout, bass, and lake herring made up most of the catch, with perch, eel, and catfish from the lesser watercourses. Among wild birds and waterfowl, the prairie chicken, a variety of grouse, was especially prized for its excellent meat.

As the terrain altered from east to west, becoming flatter and less wooded, the number of deer, elk, moose, and bear diminished, and the buffalo population rose. But nearly all the varieties of big game were found almost everywhere in the Old Northwest, and buffalo did actually roam the south shore of Lake Erie as far east as Buffalo, New York, a bit of prairieland that was well endowed with salt licks for the great beasts.

Pioneer Routes
to the Old Northwest

THERE WERE SEVERAL MEANS OF TRAVEL by which pioneers entered the Old Northwest. One of the earliest routes was via the Cumberland Gap into

Kentucky and then across the Ohio River by flatboat into the Ohio country. Soon after Ohio achieved statehood, in 1803, a more direct overland route came into use. This was the National Road, first known as the "Great National Pike," on which work was begun in 1811. It started in Maryland, passed through Columbus, Ohio, and upon its completion extended through Indiana into Illinois.

A more northerly route was via water through the Erie Canal, which was completed in 1825. The canal, over 360 miles long, joined Albany with Buffalo, connecting the Atlantic Ocean (via the Hudson River) with the Great Lakes. From Buffalo, the traveler to the Old Northwest continued by boat on Lake Erie to shore points of northern Ohio. Travel on the Erie Canal was slow, even for 1825. "Clinton's Ditch," as it was called after its planner, De Witt Clinton, was only four feet deep. The canal boats were drawn by a team of horses inching along a towpath on the shore and, as there were numerous locks, progress averaged only slightly more than one mile per hour.

For overland transportation, there was nothing to equal the Conestoga wagon, which had been developed by the Pennsylvania Germans for carrying produce to market. The large wheels kept the body of the wagon well above the rutted, uneven road surface and the wheels' broad rims made getting stuck in the mud less likely. At the same time, the Conestoga's curving, slope-sided body kept the farmer's barrels of flour and pork and kegs of lard from rolling out as the wagon jolted briskly along, drawn by teams of four to six horses.

Early American attempts at road surfacing with rough logs laid crosswise, and even with milled wooden planks, proved unsuccessful. The rough log highways were known as "corduroy roads" because of their ribbed surfaces. Although the plank roads were somewhat smoother, both decayed quickly, creating great broken gaps that were extremely dangerous. One French visitor, the Baron de Montlezun, who rode an American stagecoach in 1816, told of being "crushed, shaken, thrown about, bumped in a manner that cannot adequately be described. Every mile there is a new accident and you must go out into the mud while the damage is repaired. It is not unusual to see the coaches shattered, the passengers crippled, and the horses drowned." After 1830, the day was saved for at least some travelers in the East through the development of the steam locomotive and the subsequent building of a number of railroad lines.

Meantime, despite the hazards of the routes, pioneers eagerly embarked for the Northwest Territory. If a Conestoga wagon could not be procured for the journey, families moved west in farm wagons, in carts, on horses or mules, and very often they walked all the way to Ohio.

Settlers & Immigrants on the New Frontier

EARLY LIFE ON THE OHIO FRONTIER WAS similar to that of Kentucky—the log house in the clearing, the cornpatch among the tree stumps. Alexis de Tocqueville remarked, however, that there was one great difference. The Ohio pioneers were much more industrious and progressed far more rapidly. He attributed this to the fact that slavery was prohibited in the Northwest Territory, while in Kentucky many of the farmers, even though poor, held slaves. As a result, hard work was looked down upon and ambition was squelched for master and slave alike.

So rapid was the pace of settlement and the growth of prosperity in Ohio, that by 1830 many of the first pioneers had already sold their farms and moved farther west to Indiana and Illinois. By 1840, the frontier already stood at the border of eastern Iowa. The trail from eastern Ohio took most of the settlers to a new landscape, from woodlands to prairielands. Although the rolling prairie, dotted with only occasional clumps of trees, at first seemed discouraging for farm settlement, the "sea of grass" soon proved excellent land for wheat-growing as well as for corn and other crops.

Some of the Ohio pioneers pushed north into Michigan. "The village of Saginaw," Alexis de Tocqueville wrote in 1831, "is the last point inhabited by Europeans . . . One may regard it as an advance station, a sort of observation point which the whites have established in the midst of the Indian tribes." Yet, de Tocqueville had already seen enough of America to know that, "In but a few years these impenetrable forests will have fallen. The noise of civilization and of industry will break the silence of the Saginaw."

The rapid spread of pioneer settlements in the Old Northwest naturally brought constant conflict with the Indians. Their retreat was marked by recurrent lashings out at the westward onslaught of the new civilization. But the Indians' bouts of warfare were futile. Each time they were overpowered and pushed even farther west. De Tocqueville marveled, with bitterness, at the pioneers' philosophy that, "The true owners of this continent are those who know how to take advantage of its riches." At the same time, he commented, the new landholder attends church on Sundays "where he hears a minister of the Gospel repeat to him that all men are brothers. . . ."

One of the factors impelling the first settlers westward, driving the Indians in their wake, was the rising tide of European emigration to the New World that began in the 1830s. Often, partially developed farms could be profitably sold to the new pioneers—the German immigrants who flocked to Ohio and later moved on into Missouri, the groups from the Netherlands that settled in Michigan, the Swiss who took up life in Wisconsin, and the Scandinavians who also settled there but soon went on bravely to the harsher climates of Minnesota and the Dakotas on the Great Plains.

The reasons for the emigration of these peoples from their homelands were similar to those that had brought about the colonization of America two hundred years earlier: religious persecution, wars and revolutions, poor crops and hunger. But in the first half of the 1800s there were also new pressures. One of the far-reaching effects of the industrial revolution was progress in the field of medical science. The prolonging of human life, through the prevention and curing of diseases, had begun to cause a decline in the death rate. The birth rate, however, remained as high as before, and Europe had begun to suffer from leaping population growth. The New World was the ideal escape valve to relieve the overcrowding of Europe.

The first trickle of nineteenth-century European immigrants increased to a flow and then a torrent, as reports of life in America found their way back to Europe. One Norwegian observer, a prominent attorney named

Ole Munch Raeder, traveled via Erie Canal boat and Great Lakes steamer to Milwaukee in 1847. After making the rounds of Norwegian communities in Wisconsin, he sent home newspaper dispatches telling of the rich soil that "amply rewards one's efforts; and the raising of sheep and cattle, bee-farming, the maple sugar industry," all of which "thrive in this favored clime." Raeder added, "Hunger is an enemy from which many of our highlanders in Norway never feel safe. Just think what an impression it would make on a poor highlander's imagination to be told that some day he might eat wheat bread every day and pork at least three times a week!"

❧

Meat-and-Potatoes Eating in German Ohio

A MAJOR SPUR TO EMIGRATION FROM GERmany in the 1840s was the failure of the European potato crop (upon which so many Irish farmers were also dependent). Among the German victims of the potato famine, many sought both farming and town life in the Old Northwest.

It was Frederick the Great of Prussia who, in the 1700s, had not only suggested but had commanded that the German farmers in his realm plant potatoes, the healthful, rib-sticking food that had been discovered in the New World two centuries earlier. So it was not surprising that the Germans had developed into avid potato eaters and had devised numerous recipes for preparing this worthy tuber, which they were soon growing and eating in the New World.

Their very simplest recipe was for *Salzkartoffeln* or "salt" potatoes, boiled in salted water, steamed dry, and then dressed with melted butter and flavorful tidbits such as chopped parsley, minced onion, caraway seeds, bread crumbs, or crumbled bacon. In addition, there were recipes for *Bratkartoffeln* or fried potatoes, *Kartoffelklösse* or potato dumplings, *Kartoffelsalat* or potato salad, and *Kartoffelpuffer,* puffy, crisp-fried potato pancakes. Diced potatoes, of course, went into all sorts of soups and stews, and hot, smoothly mashed potatoes were an ingredient that found its way into chocolate cake at the hands of the German housewives of the American heartland.

German sausage-making skills, which had been developed in the Middle Ages, came right along with the new arrivals. Of all the dozens of kinds of *Wursts* or sausages that the Germans brought with them, the one that became the most popular in the United States was *Wienerwurst* or Vienna sausage, first made in that Austrian city and later named after the German city of Frankfurt. No matter what we call it today—wiener, frankfurter, or simply hot dog—this "all-American" food owes as much to the German immigration of the nineteenth century as the sauerkraut that goes on top of it or the beer that is drunk with it.

Sauerkraut had reached Germany in the Middle Ages via a lengthy route. It originated in China where the workers who constructed the Great Wall in 200 B.C. were fed a winter diet of chopped cabbage preserved in rice wine. This dish was carried westward to Russia by

Tartars and from there picked up by thirteenth-century north German sea merchants, the recipe changing somewhat in the course of its migration.

The Germans of nineteenth-century America ate their Wursts, potatoes, and sauerkraut in traditional fashion, from a plate, with bread on the side. The frankfurter-on-a-roll did not appear until late in the century, or possibly early in the 1900s, when impatient Americans began to give up on the knife and fork and turned more and more to eating stand-up snacks informally and usually in haste.

Like sauerkraut, the hamburger came to Germany from the Orient. It appears to have originated as a mound or patty of raw, scraped meat, the characteristic meal of the Tartar horsemen of the plains of central Asia. It was introduced to Russia by Tartar invaders. After sea traders brought it to Germany, people in the port city of Hamburg began to cook this raw "Tartar steak," giving us the "Hamburg steak," which was brought to nineteenth-century America by the German immigrants. The hamburger-on-a-bun, however, was probably not introduced until 1904 as one of the innovations at the St. Louis World's Fair.

Like other European immigrants to the New World, the Germans were soon eating much more meat than they had formerly. Not only was there a large amount of game available, but cattle and hogs flourished. Germans felt right at home adapting their old family recipe for *Sauerbraten,* a marinated, spiced, sweet-and-sour pot roast, to wild rabbit stew, a dish they called *Hasenpfeffer* or "peppered hare." As domestic cattle increased, the German immigrant farmers could also enjoy the *Schnitzels* of the Old World, thin slices of veal breaded and fried, sometimes topped with a fried egg, as in a dish called *Holsteiner Schnitzel.* The rest of the butchered calf

was also put to good use, with the preparation of stewed calf's tongue, roast veal, veal loaf, veal sausage, and other dishes that became specialties of German midwestern cookery.

The abundance of corn grown in Ohio and Indiana soon led to a successful hog-raising industry. Fattened animals were driven on foot from the farms to the Ohio River town of Cincinnati, which soon became a prominent meat-slaughtering center. Largely German-inhabited, Cincinnati was nicknamed "Porkopolis." It was said the packing houses were so efficient they found a use for every part of the pig but the squeal. The proximity of salt deposits along the Ohio River contributed to the rapid commercial prosperity of Cincinnati, for salt was essential to the pickling, smoking, and other curing processes connected with pork-packing.

In spite of its wealth, Cincinnati in its early days was a hodge-podge of hastily constructed shops and dwellings. There were few public services, such as garbage collection. The householders simply flung their refuse out into the middle of the road, and the pigs that wandered about the streets foraged in it for food. One foreign visitor referred to the scavenging hogs as "walking sewers."

When Frances Trollope, the mother of the famous British novelist, Anthony Trollope, moved to America in 1827 with the intention of opening a shop in Cincinnati, she was appalled at the rawness and crudity of the place. She also wrote that she had never seen "any people who appeared to live so much without amusement as the Cincinnatians. They have no public balls . . . They have no concerts. They have no dinner parties." In truth, life in Porkopolis was too busy for such fripperies, and by 1831 the disappointed Mrs. Trollope had returned to England.

As the towns of Middle America developed, they

lemon, coconut, spice, burnt sugar, black walnut, fruit, and even chocolate. Farm wife or town wife, the self-respecting midwestern hostess considered no fewer than six different kinds of cakes obligatory for a moderate-size party!

Swiss, Cornish, & Scandinavian Settlers in Wisconsin

THE TRANSFORMATION OF THE WISCONSIN wilderness into a dairying meadowland was due in large part to the efforts of Swiss pioneers who, by the 1840s, were finding the hemmed-in mountain valleys of their own country too crowded for all who wished to engage in dairy farming. On the broad Wisconsin pastures, it was possible to graze cattle for the production of milk, cream, butter, and the excellent Swiss cheeses that went into fondues and other melted cheese dishes. Especially good was the Swiss cheese-and-onion pie, a nourishing combination of milk, cream, cheese, eggs, onions, and bacon, baked brown and custardlike in a crisp pie pastry. Many people know this main-dish pie as quiche Lorraine, from France's northeastern border region with Germany. Whether Alpine or lowland in origin, it bespeaks a people with a long dairying tradition.

Quite a different vocation from dairy farming drew

immigrants from Cornwall in southwestern England to Wisconsin in the 1830s and 1840s. These newcomers were tin miners who sought better-paying work in the lead and zinc mines of the New World. The Wisconsin and nearby Michigan mines were soon worked out, and many Cornishmen drifted off to the copper mines of the Southwest. But some families remained in Wisconsin and took up farming. The Cornish left their stamp on the Old Northwest with the introduction of the Cornish pasty, a single-portion half-moon shaped pie, filled with minced meat, diced potatoes, and onions. Back home in Cornwall, these pasties had been the standard lunch taken down by the men into the tin mines.

The 1850s saw the beginnings of a large Scandinavian immigration. As many parts of the Old Northwest were by this time quite heavily populated, the first farming communities of Danes, Swedes, and Norwegians tended to cluster in Wisconsin and Minnesota. Good lands from Ohio to Iowa had long since been spoken for and were no longer cheap to buy. In the midst of this prosperous belt lay Chicago. In 1860, the still-young city boasted over 100,000 people. It was a grain-receiving center for the wheat farms of the surrounding area and was on its way to becoming a major meat-packing metropolis that would far outstrip Cincinnati.

There was, however, a more westerly frontier for the new immigrant pioneers, the Great Plains. In 1862 the government passed the Homestead Act. It offered public lands to farmers simply for settling on 160 acres of treeless sod for five years and cultivating a portion of the acreage. The catch was that the new homesteading lands lay in what was then known as the "Great American Desert," an apparent wasteland, not of sand but of desolation.

❦

Buffalo Hunters & Sodbusters of the Great Plains

OUT WHERE THE PLAINS BEGAN, THE ROLL-ing prairie flattened into a bleak, treeless, waterless expanse that swept westward from the state of Kansas, ascending gradually to the foothills of the Rockies. Although the region had been crossed by explorers, trappers, California forty-niners, and wagon trains heading for the lush, green Oregon country, no one had yet attempted settlement there. For this windswept land of short, tough-rooted buffalo grass held many natural terrors including blizzards and tornadoes, stampeding buffalo and plagues of grasshoppers, and nights filled with the howling of coyotes and the throaty screams of cougars. In the early 1860s it was, in fact, still the home of Indian buffalo hunters.

The Siouan Crow, Mandan, and Kansa tribes, the Pawnee and Arikara of the Caddoan family, and the Cheyenne of the Algonquian all inhabited the region that later became the states of Kansas, Nebraska, South Dakota, and North Dakota. These Indians engaged little in agriculture, partly because they lacked suitable tools of metal for breaking the thick matted covering of the plains, but also because they had found that they could live almost exclusively off the buffalo. Before the Spanish brought horses to the Americas in the 1500s, the Plains Indians had hunted the buffalo on foot. Skillfully, they had constructed huge traps of piled up stones and then stampeded the herds into them, making the great beasts easy targets for their arrows.

In addition to supplying meat and tallow, the buffalo gave the Indians hides for tepees, robes, and moccasins. Ribs and horns could be carved into knives, scrapers, and other implements; the animals' tendons supplied sewing thread. And the dried buffalo chips were fuel for cooking and heating fires.

The meat of a buffalo kill was not all consumed at once. Some of it was preserved for future use by slicing it into paper-thin strips, which were then dried in the sun or over the smoke of a fire. The meat was then known as jerk or jerky, from the word *charqui,* which the Spanish had given to this American Indian product. Jerky, although leathery and not very tasty, could be chewed on dry as an emergency ration. It could also be pounded to a powder and cooked in water, sometimes with a little cornmeal.

Pemmican was another long-keeping Indian food, combining shredded jerked meat, dried wild berries, and buffalo tallow, formed into small cakes and stored in buffalo-skin bags. The Indians of the eastern woodlands had prepared their jerky from venison, and the technique had been adopted by the early scouts and trappers of the New World.

The Civil War gave the Indian hunters of the Great Plains a few years of grace before the final takeover of their lands by the encroaching civilization from the east. Already threatened by the invasion of professional white buffalo-hunters, the Plains Indians' way of life changed forever with the close of the war. Peace brought the completion of the transcontinental railroad in 1869 and the migration of the homesteaders to their one-time hunting grounds. By the early 1880s, the days of the wild buffalo hunt were over, and the Indians of the Great Plains were doomed to the enforced idleness and demoralization of life on the reservation.

The Scandinavians, Germans, and other immigrants who settled the plains and the American farm families who decided to move west and try their luck on the free public lands encountered a frontier that no pioneer on the continent had experienced before. The almost total lack of wood meant that houses had to be built of the very same virgin sod that the homesteading "sodbusters" had to break in order to sow their crops and dig the wells, hundreds of feet deep, that would supply the necessary irrigation.

Soon the featureless plains began to sprout an occasional cabin built of rectangular blocks of grass, tangled roots, and clinging earth, jokingly tagged as "Nebraska marble." Beside the sod house or "soddy" rose an exceptionally tall windmill, its twirling sails designed to catch the high winds of the plains and to drive the pump that brought water up from deep underground.

"Nasty" was probably the word most frequently used to describe the interior of the sod house. The floors, walls, and ceiling were of packed earth, the latter supported by a few precious wooden poles and rafters. Bugs of all sorts emerged from the walls, field mice ran rampant within, soil sifted down on one's head in dry weather, and mud rolled down in wet. Many families built dugout dwellings, half sod house, half earthen cave, in the sides of small embankments in areas known as benchlands. Often the sod roof sprouted grass and even flowers, inviting the family cow atop the dwelling. When that happened, it was not unusual for the entire roof to collapse, drowning the one-room interior and its occupants in a cascade of crumbling earth.

After six or seven years, the sod dwelling needed re-

building. If the pioneer family had worked hard and been lucky with its crops, the new house might be built of wood this time, with lumber hauled from the east. Or perhaps enough wood could be obtained for a floor. One visitor to the Great Plains, a representative of a Boston farm mortgage company named Seth K. Humphrey, wrote of stopping for a meal at a sod house where the family told him how they desperately hoped each year "to have enough money to buy lumber for a floor." Humphrey described how "Numberless sweepings had left the stove and the table a few inches above the rest of the clay floor level, and this made it a bit awkward with the chairs. . . ."

Many pioneer families were afflicted with bad luck on the plains—drought, poor soil, prairie fires, the well run dry, livestock destroyed by blizzards or wild animals, illness, unbearable loneliness. Ruefully, they abandoned their holdings, packed their wagons, and headed back east. Often, perhaps as a warning to others, the defeated homesteader attached a sign, roughly lettered, to the side of the wagon: "Goin' back to my wife's folks." Others more jauntily announced: "In God we trusted, in Kansas we busted!"

For those who prospered, however, life on the plains eventually became as comfortable as that in the Old Northwest, except for the more severe climate. The introduction of a variety of winter wheat known as Turkey Red was to help turn the region into America's breadbasket, a distinction it still holds today. This type of wheat, so well suited to the plains' soil and climate, was brought to Kansas by a group of German Mennonite immigrants who had been living in Russia and growing it there with success. The settlers of the plains soon learned that tree-planting helped to enrich the soil and conserve moisture. The first Arbor Day, in fact, was observed in Nebraska in April 1872.

Among the able survivors of pioneering on the Great Plains were many Scandinavian families. Although fish was far less common in their diet than in their sea-girt homelands, there were vegetables, meats, and dairy products, and of course wheat and other grains for the breads, pancakes, pastries, coffee cakes, and cookies that were traditional in the Scandinavian cuisine.

Christmas was an especially warm time. The sod house, despite its drawbacks, was well insulated against the harsh outdoors, and the kitchen fire glowed with burning corncobs or dried cornstalks, a substitute for hard-to-come-by wood. Careful hoarding of raisins, candied fruits, nuts, sugar, and well-liked spices like cardamom seed and anise seed meant that a Swedish family could have a yule bread asparkle with candied fruit or a frosted Christmas tea ring studded with nuts. Best of all, there might be an assortment of Swedish Christmas cookies, particularly the beloved buttery *spritz* cookies that could be shaped into stars, wreaths, crowns, and even Christmas trees.

The holiday was a suitable time for reflection and for thanksgiving. The pioneer family of the plains gave thanks for another summer's harvest safely delivered, for the winter wheat sowed snugly beneath the snow ready for sprouting in the spring, for the hard-earned rewards of having established a foothold and brought forth a living from the forbidding terrain and climate of the Great American Desert.

Recipes from

the Old Northwest and the Great Plains

⊷ KARTOFFELPUFFER

2 cups finely grated raw potato (about 4 large
   potatoes)
1 small onion, finely grated
1 teaspoon salt
  dash white pepper
2 tablespoons dried bread crumbs, cracker meal,
   or flour
1 egg white, beaten stiff
  oil for frying

After grating potato and onion, combine and let stand
about 10 minutes. Pour off any excess liquid that ac-
cumulates. Add all remaining ingredients, carefully
folding in beaten egg white last.

Heat oil, about ¼-inch deep, in a 10-inch skillet.
When sizzling hot, add potato mixture from a tablespoon, forming oval patties about 4 inches long. Fry at
medium-high heat until crisp, deep golden-brown on
bottom. Turn with spatula and fry other side. Place
cooked potato pancakes on paper toweling to absorb
excess fat. Pancakes may then be kept warm in a 250-
degree oven while second batch is frying.

Kartoffelpuffer are especially good with pot roast and gravy. Chilled applesauce is an excellent accompaniment to the hot pancakes, with or without a meat course. This recipe makes about 10 pancakes.

◄ξ *HOLLANDSCHE APPEL KOEK*

1½   cups sifted all-purpose flour
2   teaspoons baking powder
¼   teaspoon salt
⅔   cup sugar
½   cup butter or margarine (¼ pound or 1 stick)
1   egg, lightly beaten
    milk (about ½ cup)
½   teaspoon vanilla extract

Apple Topping

2 ½   cups pared apples cut in wedges about ¼-inch
        thick*
¼   cup sugar
1   teaspoon cinnamon
⅛   teaspoon nutmeg
⅛   teaspoon salt
1   tablespoon butter or margarine

Preheat oven to 375 degrees Fahrenheit. Combine flour, baking powder, salt, and sugar and sift into a medium-large mixing bowl. Cut in butter or margarine with a pastry blender or two knives worked crisscross until shortening is the size of peas. Pour beaten egg into measuring cup and add enough milk to make ¾ cup liquid. Add, with vanilla, to dry ingredients and stir mix-

*Use tart, crisp apples such as Greenings or McIntosh.

ture just until well blended. Consistency will not be smooth.

Turn batter into a greased 8 x 8 x 2 or 9 x 9 x 2 baking pan and spread evenly. Arrange apple slices atop batter in rows, slices overlapping slightly. Combine remaining ingredients for topping, cutting in butter or working it with fingertips until mixture is crumbly. Sprinkle over apple slices. Bake at 375 degrees for 35 minutes. Serve this Dutch apple cake slightly warm if possible. Makes 8–10 servings.

⤚ SWISS CHEESE-AND-ONION PIE

1	9-inch pie shell*
6	strips bacon, fried crisp and crumbled
2	tablespoons butter or margarine
2	medium-size onions, sliced in thin rings
1½	cups coarsely shredded Swiss cheese
4	eggs, beaten
⅔	cup milk
⅔	cup light cream**
1	tablespoon prepared Dijon or mild, herb-seasoned mustard
½	teaspoon salt
¼	teaspoon white pepper
¼	teaspoon grated nutmeg

---

*Prepare pie shell as in recipe for Pecan Pie, or use commercial mix, or commercially prepared shell, as suggested.

** If unavailable, use 1⅓ cups "half-and-half" instead of milk and cream. Dish can also be prepared with 1⅓ cups milk, omitting cream.

Preheat oven to 425 degrees Fahrenheit. Prick pie shell lightly all over with fork. Brush all of inside with a little of the beaten egg. Bake shell at 425 degrees for 5 to 8 minutes, or until set but not browned. Remove from oven and place on rack to cool. Reduce oven heat to 375 degrees.

Fry bacon and pour off excess fat from pan. Add butter or margarine to same skillet and bring to sizzling. Add onion rings and sauté until limp and golden-brown. Layer crumbled bacon, cooled onion rings, and shredded Swiss cheese on bottom of cooled pie shell.

In a medium-large bowl, combine eggs, milk, cream, and seasonings. Beat with wire whisk to blend well. Pour carefully atop ingredients in pie shell. Bake at 375 degrees for 40 minutes or until pie is golden-brown, puffed, and firm in center. Remove from oven and cool ten minutes before cutting.

Serve Swiss cheese-and-onion pie in pie-shaped wedges. A crisp mixed green salad or a raw spinach salad with a light oil-and-vinegar dressing is all the accompaniment needed. Left-over pie can be reheated in oven at 325 degrees. Cut into wedges before reheating. Serves 6–8.

SPRITZ COOKIES

½   cup butter (¼ pound or 1 stick)
2   hard-cooked egg yolks, put through medium-coarse strainer
¼   cup sugar
½   teaspoon almond extract
1   cup sifted all-purpose flour

Preheat oven to 375 degrees Fahrenheit.

Allow butter to soften slightly. In a medium-size mixing bowl, mash with back of wooden spoon until creamy. Blend in egg yolks, sugar, and almond extract. Add flour gradually, mixing thoroughly.

Mixture should be firm, yet soft enough to force through cookie press, following directions for making stars, snowflakes, wreaths, Christmas trees, and other designs. Lacking a cookie press, the mixture may be rolled into ¾-inch balls, placed 2 inches apart on an ungreased cookie sheet, and flattened to about ¼-inch thickness with the bottom of a glass lightly dipped in flour.

Decorate cookies with colored sugar or sprinkles, bits of candied cherry, green citron, or other glacé fruit. To make colored sugar, mix a drop of red or green food coloring into ¼ cup sugar and stir thoroughly.

Bake spritz cookies for about 10 minutes, or just until light brown around the edges. This recipe makes about 3 dozen cookies.

Along the Santa Fe Trail to the Southwest

"THE TOWN WAS CROWDED. A MUL-titude of shops had sprung up to furnish the emigrants and Santa Fe traders with necessaries for their journey; and there was an incessant hammering and banging from a dozen blacksmiths' sheds, where the heavy wagons were being repaired, and the horses and oxen shod." So wrote Francis Parkman, a young Bostonian anxious to sample western travel, in the spring of 1846. The town he was writing about was Independence, Missouri, an outpost of civilization on the eastern edge of the Great Plains.

Independence, adjacent to Kansas City, was the starting point of the Santa Fe Trail, an 800-mile caravan route that crossed the plains in a southwesterly direction and culminated in the town of Santa Fe, high in the Sangre de Cristo Range of the southern Rockies. The journey across an oceanlike expanse of buffalo grass into an arid, sun-baked landscape of steep-sided mesas and towering buttes, pocked with stiff-armed cactus plants, spiky yucca, and shrublike mesquite trees, was like a passage into a foreign country. And indeed this was a foreign country, for much of what we today regard as the American Southwest—the states of Texas,

New Mexico, and Arizona—belonged to Spain from the earliest days of exploration and, after 1821, to Mexico.

In Mexican territory south of the Rio Grande, a blending of American Indian and Spanish cultures had begun to take place as early as 1519, when the Spanish *conquistadores* under Cortez set foot upon the North American mainland and encountered the Aztecs, one of the most advanced agricultural peoples of the New World.

However, many of the foods that they and the island inhabitants of the West Indies grew were oddities in European eyes. Maize, or Indian corn, had been a revelation to Columbus and his men when they first found it growing on the island of Cuba. The variety of beans— red, pink, black, cream-colored, and even spotted, or *pinto* as the Spanish called them—was astonishing compared to the standard broad bean of Europe. In addition, there was the tomato, suspect though it was as an edible at first, the sweet potato, numerous kinds of peppers ranging in taste from mild to fiery, the vanilla bean, the cacao bean from which chocolate was derived, and the native American turkey. Having no sugar or other effective sweetener, the Aztecs combined chocolate, in its bitter state, with spices and herbs to make a dark, pungent sauce for flavoring roast turkey. Even today, chicken or turkey with *mole* (mo-lay) sauce is a Mexican specialty that can also be found in the Mexican-influenced states just north of the border.

Indian Foods of the American Southwest

SOON AFTER THEIR CONQUEST OF THE Aztecs, Spanish explorers began to investigate the region farther to the north that was later to become part of the United States. There they found a much poorer and more loosely organized Indian civilization that had once dwelt in multistoried apartments carved out of the shelflike sides of tall cliffs and canyon walls. By the 1500s, possibly as a result of prolonged drought or because of persistent raiding by nomadic Apache and Navaho peoples, these corn-growers had relocated to small, scattered villages or *pueblos* where they lived in adobe huts adjacent to their fields. The Spanish named these peaceful toilers Pueblo Indians, although they belonged to various tribes including the Hopi, Zuñi, Pima, Papago, and Tano.

The area they inhabited was drier, rockier, and less fertile than the great bowl-shaped valley of the Aztecs far to the south, and it offered a fairly spartan diet. Besides the basic triad of cultivated foods, corn, beans, and squash, the Pueblos gathered the beans of the wild mesquite, the flat oval seeds of the low-growing *piñon* pine, and the thorny prickly pear, fruit of the cactus. Mesquite beans could be ground between stones into a flour and mixed with water to bake into mesquite bean cakes. *Pinole* was a dish that combined dried maize, mesquite beans, and various parched grains and seeds.

The Pueblo Indians ate meat only occasionally. They

kept flocks of the wild turkey, which they had domesticated, and they snared rabbit and other small game. Large game animals, like mountain lion, deer, antelope, and bear, were the prey of the Apaches and other hunting tribes who sometimes ventured out onto the Great Plains in search of buffalo. The hunting Indians of the Southwest seldom grew any food of their own, preferring to commandeer it from their agriculturalist neighbors.

⋙⋘

The Culinary Gifts of the Spanish

THE FOODS TRANSPLANTED TO THE NEW World after the arrival of the first Europeans added flavor, variety, color, and nutriment to the basically bland and starchy Indian diet, enlivened only by the bite of hot chili peppers. Onions, garlic, and olives gave piquancy to corn-based dishes. Wheat and rice extended the choice of grains beyond corn. Sugar meant that chocolate and vanilla could become fully developed flavorings. Oranges, lemons, grapes, apricots, and other fruits contributed tang and succulence to the cuisine. And the introduction of cattle, sheep, goats, and chickens put milk, cheese, eggs, and much more meat into the diet of the Indian farming peoples.

In 1609, the Spanish established a mission-fortress at Santa Fe and made it the capital of the Spanish-held province that surrounded it, later to become the state of New Mexico. Gradually Spanish priests spread through the region, establishing small missionary churches as far east as Texas and as far west as California. Their purpose was to bring Christianity to the Indians by developing mission farms on which the Indians worked the fields in exchange for religious education and a paternalistic concern for their welfare. The earliest citrus groves, vineyards, and olive orchards of the Southwest were Indian-cultivated under the direction of the Spanish padres. In areas unsuited to agriculture, many Spanish estate owners established ranches, taking on Indians to oversee the cattle and sheep. These Indian ranch hands were the original cowboys of the New World.

The first cattle of the Southwest were of a strain developed in the Andalusian region of Spain. They were known as longhorns, and as they did not yield very choice beef—especially after their rough American diet of cactus and other thorny pasturage—they were raised chiefly for their hides and tallow.

Tough, stringy longhorn beef did become acceptable, however, when it was finely diced for a *chili con carne* (chili with meat). This was a stew of beef, onions, garlic, and sometimes red beans, seasoned with a fairly hot chili powder. This dish represented the wedding of Indian and Spanish ingredients, and became a classic in the American Southwest. Another dish that literally put the longhorn steers of New Mexico and west Texas into a Spanish soup was *sopa de albóndigas,* an onion-and-garlic-seasoned beef or chicken broth with flavorful meatballs (*albóndigas*) floating in it.

Other results of the coming together of Spanish and Indian cuisines were the variations on the theme of the *tortilla.* The Spanish-named tortilla, meaning "little cake," was really the bread of the Mexican and Central

American Indians before the arrival of the Europeans. Unlike the cornbread of most of the Indians living north of the Rio Grande, these thin flexible cakes were made from a corn paste known as *masa* rather than from a mixture of dry cornmeal and water. Masa was prepared from the wet kernels of dried, cooked corn mashed to a smooth doughy mass on a flat stone called a *metate*. The Indian women to whom this daily chore belonged were magically skilled at shaping large circular wafers of dough from chunks of masa and then toasting the rounds to pale brown on a large flat pan over an open fire.

The resulting tortillas served as edible scoops for the boiled *frijoles* (beans) that were customarily eaten three times a day, sprinkled with a little roasted chili pepper to counteract their blandness. The introduction of European ingredients led to such tasty developments as the *enchilada,* a rolled-up tortilla encasing such fillings as hot sauce (mainly water and ground, dried chili peppers), grated cheese, chopped green olives, minced onion, frijoles, and shredded chicken or ground meat or sausage, the whole topped with a splash of more hot sauce and crisp shredded lettuce. Enchilada fillings may be found in any number of combinations. The same is true of the fillings for the *taco,* a tortilla folded in half, filled, and fried crisp like a turnover, and the *tostada,* a tortilla fried flat and heaped with savory ingredients.

Either masa or cornmeal makes a cereal-paste filling for another Indian dish, the *tamal,* or "bundle," which is wrapped in cornhusks and cooked by steaming. The addition of Old World ingredients, like a seasoned chicken or pork filling dabbed atop the cereal paste, made the Indian *tamales* both tastier and more nourishing.

Even the plain boiled beans of the Indians underwent some changes after the arrival of the Europeans. Not only did they appear in chili con carne but also as *frijoles fritos,* cooked beans mashed with a little liquid and fried to a thick mush, and as *frijoles refritos,* crisp-edged refried beans seasoned with salt, garlic, and chili powder. Spanish-introduced rice was also incorporated into the Indian diet. And, like the Spanish-Indian versions of tortillas, tamales, and frijoles, it became popular on both sides of the Rio Grande, particularly in a Spanish-derived but chili-seasoned dish called *arroz con pollo,* or rice with chicken.

At the time of the founding of Santa Fe, in 1609, the British were just settling Jamestown, Virginia, thousands of miles to the east. Between the two early outposts of European civilization lay a vast wilderness. Therefore it was not until the 1820s, as part of the pioneer movement westward, that Anglo-American families first began to settle in east Texas. They chose the area along the Gulf Coast, for the soil and climate there presented good opportunities for rice- and cotton-growing.

Another group of pioneers, who penetrated more deeply into the Southwest at about that time, were the Santa Fe traders, venturing into Spanish-held territory first on pack horses and later in wagons via the Santa Fe Trail. Setting out each spring from Independence, Missouri, these intrepid merchants made a tidy profit, barring the hazards of the trail. They supplied the Spanish and the Indians with manufactured goods and brought back hides, mules, horses, and gold and silver from the mines of Mexico.

In 1848, as a result of the Mexican War, the Southwest became part of the United States. The chain of events leading up to this development included Mexico's revolt against Spain in 1821, followed by Texas' declaration of independence from Mexico in 1836. Texas became a state in 1845 and continued to attract farming families as well as other settlers who took up cattle ranching. However, the highly scenic but more desert-like country to the west attracted only a trickle of miners, ranchers, and cowhands. So sparse did the populations of New Mexico and Arizona remain, even after 1848, that neither was eligible for statehood until 1912.

Yet it was this slow infiltration of easterners and their adaptation to the long dominant Mexican traditions of the region that helped to preserve the vivid culinary character of this portion of the Southwest.

Oklahoma Chuckwagon Days

DURING THE CIVIL WAR YEARS, THE TEXAS rangelands became heavily stocked with cattle. Some of the new ranchers of the 1850s had brought herds of English shorthorns and Herefords west with them, as both were superior in beef-producing quality to the half-wild Spanish longhorns. Whatever their breed, the animals flourished on the Texas grasses. Yet they could not be safely or conveniently shipped to market while hostilities between the states continued.

Once the war ended, a great era of railroad building began, and it became possible to transport the animals from America's new cattlelands to packing houses and consumers in St. Louis, Chicago, and points east via the recently completed rail lines. However, a distance of some 600 to 700 miles lay between the Texas range and the railheads in the Kansas "cow towns" of Wichita, Abilene, and Dodge City. For this portion of the journey, the cattle had to be driven on the hoof, an operation known as the "long drive," from which sprang some of the most colorful cowboy lore of nineteenth century America.

The perils of the trail were considerable. The herds frequently numbered close to 3000, and the most serious danger was that of a stampede, for the Texas longhorns were a temperamental and unpredictable lot. The cowhands had to be wary, skillful, and rugged. Other hazards of the weeks' or even months' long trek were Indian raids, attacks by rustlers or wild animals, and the spread of cattle diseases like the dreaded tick fever. Yet the journey could not be hurried, for the more slowly the beasts moved across northern Texas, the territory of Oklahoma, and southwestern Kansas, and the more thoroughly they fed on the rich grasses of the summer plains, the fatter they were when they arrived at the cow town markets to be weighed up and purchased by cattle buyers and shipped east in freight cars.

On the trail, food had to be provided for the trail boss and the dozen or so cowhands he had carefully selected, so the choice of an able cook or "pot wrangler," usually dubbed "cookie" by the rest of the men, was a serious matter. Unlike their charges, the cowboys could not be expected to eat off the country. Their hours were long and their duties exhausting. Even after making camp at night, they usually bedded the cattle down and sang them to sleep, lulling them with mournful ballads that eventually built into a well-known repertory of cowboy songs.

The remarkable rolling kitchen out of which the pot

wrangler did his cooking was called a chuckwagon. Colonel Charles Goodnight, a pioneer cattleman of the Texas Panhandle, is credited with having invented it. Actually, the chuckwagon was an ordinary-looking covered wagon with a tall box that had a large drop door built onto the back of it. The box was a traveling pantry with shelves holding staples like flour, cornmeal, rice, salt, sugar, coffee, dried beans, lard, raisins, cured pork, and other nonperishables.

When the trail outfit came to a halt, the cook simply let down the hinged drop door of the pantry and, supported by a couple of hinged-on legs, it converted into a work table for mixing biscuits, cornbread, and hotcakes, and preparing stews, beans, and coffee. Food was cooked over an open fire in one of cookie's huge kettles or iron skillets. Steaks from the steers slaughtered en route were coated with flour and salt and fried in sizzling beef fat or lard. "Chuckwagon stew" consisted of chunks of beef plus parts like tongue, heart, liver, kidneys, and brains, well seasoned with onions, salt, and chili powder. Occasionally the monotony of beef would be varied with venison, wild turkey, prairie chicken, or even buffalo.

The nearest thing to a vegetable dish was dried beans, usually the pinto beans of the Southwest. Oddly speckled, like birds' eggs, with spots of brown on beige, the beans turned a rich, warm, all-over brown when cooked. This food was the heritage of the Indians, passed on to the cowboys of the Southwest just as the first Indian cowhands had taught the skills of the *vaquero,* in roping and branding cattle, to the newcomers from the east. The dish known as "chuckwagon beans," eaten frequently on the long cattle drives, reflected both Indian and Spanish influences, for it included onions, garlic, and salt pork or bacon, as well as chili powder. The

cooking time could be reduced somewhat by soaking the beans in water first, although long, slow cooking guaranteed firmer beans. Chuckwagon beans made a meal in themselves, the creamy bean liquid mopped up with freshly-made biscuits "baked" over an open fire in a well-heated, covered iron pot.

Trail biscuits were made to rise by the use of sourdough "starter," a fermented mixture that produced gas bubbles and so acted as a substitute for yeast. The trail cook's greatest treasure was his small wooden cask of sourdough that he kept warm and well-replenished, even taking it to bed with him on cold nights. Once a cask of sourdough got working—through the addition of sugar or molasses to flour, water, and salt—it could go on for years. So each time the chuckwagon cook added some sourdough starter to his biscuit dough or hotcake batter, he made sure to add some more flour, water, and salt to the cask to ferment. Gold prospectors in California and, after the turn of the century, in Alaska also carried sourdough starters with them. Alaskan miners even came to be nicknamed "sourdoughs."

The biggest cooking problem on the trail, beyond that of keeping the water cask well filled, was finding adequate fuel. Twigs, dried grasses, and any other dry vegetable matter that would burn was carefully collected as the outfit moved along. But often the cooking fire had to be made with dried cow chips, just as the Indians of the Great Plains made their cooking fires with dried buffalo chips.

Coffee was a round-the-clock beverage for the trail gang, and a pot was kept hot, sitting in the embers of the fire, all through the night as the cowhands came off their watches. Meals were pretty much the same whether they were breakfast, lunch, or dinner; fried steak, stew, or beans was as likely at one as at the other.

Desserts were rare, but sometimes cookie would prepare "spotted pup," a dish of cooked rice and raisins sweetened with brown sugar.

The heyday of the long cattle drives across Oklahoma, from Texas to Kansas, lasted less than twenty years. As the homesteaders came onto the Great Plains during the 1860s and 1870s, more and more buffalo grass was plowed under for the planting of wheat fields. The invention of barbed wire in 1874 gave the homesteaders a means of fencing in their fields and, at the same time, fencing out the herds of cattle passing through to graze. Skirmishes often took place between the cattlemen and the farmers, and the former sometimes cut the metal fences claiming that the barbs injured their cattle. By the early 1880s, the days of the open range were clearly numbered.

Oklahoma, a plains state that is geographically part of the Southwest, was the last to be homesteaded. Its territory had been part of the Louisiana Purchase, and early in the century it had been set aside as a home for the eastern Indian tribes that had been pushed ever westward by the pioneer settlers. As homesteading took its toll of other rich pasturage areas, cattlemen began to look enviously at unspoiled Oklahoma. Wheat and cotton farmers, too, cast anxious glances toward this last frontier.

The Indians argued bitterly against the breaking of the treaties in which the United States government had guaranteed them the independent administration of their lands in Oklahoma for "as long as grass shall grow and rivers run." But in 1889, despite their protests, some of the choicest land in Oklahoma was opened to settlers on a first-come, first-served basis, and a frantic land rush to stake out claims was on.

Soon after, additional lands were opened. The In-

dians' holdings were steadily compressed, their independence was eroded, and their interests were gradually
sacrificed to those of the state's rapidly growing white
population.

For the cattlemen, the Oklahoma land settlements
were not nearly the tragedy they were for the Indians.
The 1880s saw the building of railroad lines directly into
Texas, eliminating the need for walking Texas livestock
to Kansas cow towns. Although the colorful days of the
long cattle drives were over, the long-term prosperity of
the ranchers of the Southwest was pretty well assured.

Recipes from
the Southwest

⋅§ SOPA DE ALBONDIGAS

2 tablespoons olive oil or salad oil, or 1 tablespoon each
1 small onion, finely diced
1 clove garlic, put through garlic press
1 cup skinned, cubed tomatoes, either fresh or
canned variety, well-drained*
4 cups beef broth, home-made or canned, or prepared with 5 beef bouillon cubes and 4 cups
boiling water

Albóndigas (*Meat Balls*)
½ pound ground beef
2 tablespoons uncooked rice
1 egg, beaten
½ teaspoon salt
½ teaspoon chili powder
2 teaspoons minced fresh parsley

Heat oil in a 4-quart soup kettle. Add onion and garlic
and cook, stirring with a wooden spoon, until pale gold.
Add tomatoes and beef broth. Simmer 10 minutes.

---

*To skin fresh tomatoes, follow instructions in recipe for
Burgoo.

Combine ingredients for *albóndigas* and shape into approximately twenty one-inch balls. Add meat balls to simmering soup, cover, and cook gently about 25 minutes or until rice in meat balls is tender. Check seasoning, adding salt and chili powder if necessary. Makes 4–6 servings.

◄§ *BEEF ENCHILADAS*

4	tablespoons corn oil or other salad oil
1	medium-size onion, cut in ¼-inch dice
1	clove garlic, put through garlic press
¾	pound ground round steak or other lean beef
½	teaspoon salt
3	tablespoons sliced green or black olives
	Mexican-style chili-seasoned "hot" sauce (commercially prepared, sold in cans)*
1¾	cups coarsely grated sharp Cheddar cheese
1	cup shredded crisp lettuce
	chopped onions (optional)
8	tortillas (commercially prepared, sold in cans)

Heat 2 tablespoons of the oil in a medium-size frying pan. Add diced onion and pressed garlic and sauté until pale gold. Add ground meat gradually, crumbling it with the fingers to prevent large clumps forming as it cooks. Stir contents of pan with wooden spoon until meat loses its pink color. Add salt and olives and set aside. Have ready the chili-seasoned sauce, grated cheese, shredded lettuce, and chopped onions, if using.

---

*Mexican sauces are sometimes sold in "mild" and "hot" versions. The "mild" sauce is sufficiently peppery for most tastes. Ordinary tomato-base "chili sauce" is not a correct substitute.

To a small frying pan, add a scant teaspoon of the remaining oil and heat. Add one tortilla and fry it a few seconds, just until it becomes flexible. Turn with spatula and quickly fry other side. Remove tortilla, drain it lightly on a paper towel, and spread top with about half a teaspoon of the sauce. Put about one-eighth of the meat mixture and two to three tablespoons of the grated cheese in the center of the tortilla. Roll it up and place it in a 10-inch pie plate or other shallow baking dish. Set oven to 350 degrees Fahrenheit.

Repeat with remaining tortillas. If fried too long, tortillas will become too crisp to roll (they then become tostadas and may be topped with the filling ingredients and served flat). Enchiladas may unroll or open up partially in baking dish, especially if tortillas are small in diameter.

When baking dish is full, sprinkle enchiladas with several teaspoons of the sauce, cover with remaining grated cheese, and place in 350 degree oven for 10 to 15 minutes, or until cheese melts and enchiladas are hot. Cover with shredded lettuce and, if desired, chopped onions. Serve at once.

A marinated bean salad or an avocado-and-grapefruit salad is a good accompaniment to a main course of beef enchiladas. Makes 3–4 servings.

⋖§ *CHUCKWAGON BEANS*

2   cups pinto beans, or small red beans (about 1 pound)

5   cups cold water

½   pound meaty, thick-sliced, raw bacon, cut in 2-inch squares

1   large onion, diced fine

1   large clove garlic, put through garlic press

2½   teaspoons chili powder
2   teaspoons salt

Wash and pick over beans. Place in heavy 4-quart cooking pot, preferably cast aluminum or enameled cast iron. Add the water. It should reach two inches above the level of the beans. Bring to a boil and simmer gently, tightly covered, for 1½ to 2 hours, or until beans are just becoming tender. Check to make sure that beans are not sticking to bottom of pot or becoming too dry. If liquid cooks away too quickly, add a little more water from time to time.

Add bacon, onion, garlic, chili powder, and salt. Blend in gently with wooden spoon so as not to mash beans. Cook, covered, one hour longer or until beans are very tender but still holding their shape. Check seasoning, adding more salt and chili powder if necessary. Chuckwagon beans are excellent as a main dish along with a shredded-carrot-and-raisin salad or a green salad, or they may be served as an accompaniment to meat. To reheat leftover beans, add enough water to prevent sticking and to give a creamy consistency. Makes 6–8 servings.

◄§ *SPOTTED PUP*

½   cup raw long-grain rice
⅓   cup dark brown sugar, firmly packed
4   cups milk (you may use 3 cups milk plus 1 cup
       light cream or 1 cup "half-and-half")
½   cup raisins

Measure rice, place in a fine strainer or sieve and rinse well with cold water. In a medium-large saucepan, about 2-quart size, combine drained rice and remaining ingredients.

Bring contents of saucepan to simmering. Watch pot *very* carefully, controlling heat so that milk does not boil over. Simmer mixture, uncovered, for about 45 minutes, or until rice grains are tender and most of milk is absorbed.

Turn off heat, cover saucepan, and let it stand on warm range unit for about 15 minutes. Serve spotted pup warm. Makes 6–8 servings.

Over the Rockies
to the Far West

E̲V̲E̲N̲ B̲E̲F̲O̲R̲E̲ T̲H̲E̲ F̲I̲R̲S̲T̲ P̲I̲O̲N̲E̲E̲R̲S̲ had begun to inch their way across the southern mountains into the Kentucky country, Americans were haunted with the thought of finding a quick route to the "Great River of the West." They visualized that mythical waterway as a broad stream connecting the eastern mountains to the Pacific Ocean and giving the young United States direct access to the China trade and to the riches of the Indies originally sought by Columbus.

The Lewis and Clark Expedition did indeed reach the Pacific coast late in the year 1805, but the experiences of that intrepid party proved that no all-water route to the Far West existed. Instead the explorers encountered the frozen, windswept plains of North Dakota, where they spent the winter of 1804–5, the rugged heights of the Rockies, which they crossed via an 8000-foot pass in central Idaho, and finally the treacherous rapids, often requiring portage, of a series of turbulent rivers that gushed and tumbled westward from the Continental Divide.

Beyond the buffalo-inhabited Great Plains, food became increasingly scarce. Captain Clark described his first meeting in the Rockies with a grizzly bear, a "verry large and a turrible looking animal, which we found verry hard to kill. This animal is the largest of the carnivorous kind I ever saw."

So dangerous and intimidating were the bears, moose, and wild bighorn sheep of the Rockies that jerky, prepared in advance from elk and buffalo meat, saw the party through most of the rigors of its mountain passage. The Indian woman Sacajawea, who helped the travelers make friendly contact with her own people, the Shoshone, and later with the Nez Percé of northern Idaho, managed to obtain some food en route. As the wife of a French Canadian trader on the expedition, Sacajawea served as interpreter and guide all the way to the Pacific, and even bore a child in the course of the journey.

The trek from Idaho through Washington to the shores of the Pacific was via the Clearwater, Snake, and Columbia Rivers. To Lewis and Clark and their companions, the river country was a dismal disappointment because of its meager supply of game. They soon discovered that the Chinook and other Indian tribes along the Columbia lived principally on salmon, either fresh or dried, a steady diet of which did not appeal at all to the explorers. Small game and waterfowl were available, but the party soon developed a preference for the meat of dogs, which they bought from the Indians and which the men declared to be "sweet." Horseflesh was also preferred to fish.

The Indians' catch of salmon took place during the spring and fall spawning seasons, when the great fish hurled themselves upstream from the Pacific to lay their eggs. At those times of year, the Columbia River shallows were so thick with the gleaming bodies of countless salmon that the Indians of the Northwest simply speared or clubbed them to death from their canoes or from the river bank. To ensure a year round supply, some of the catch was cut into thin strips and dried for jerky, exactly as the Eastern and Plains Indians prepared jerky from venison or buffalo meat. Dried salmon could also be pounded into powdery flakes and mixed with dried berries and a flour of pounded dried roots for a kind of "fish pemmican," resembling the pemmican of the meat-eating Indians. As wild berries, edible roots, seeds, and nuts were all fairly plentiful in the Pacific Northwest, the Indians of the region almost completely ignored agriculture.

Despite the success of their mission in reaching the Pacific, Lewis and Clark reported spending a miserable Christmas of 1805 in the fort they had constructed at the point where the Columbia River met the sea. On the northern bank of the river lay what is today the state of Washington. To the south lay present-day Oregon, a region where elk were reported to be more plentiful and into which the party organized hunting expeditions. The area surrounding the fort, however, was cheerless. The Pacific coastal weather was wet and chilly, the ceaseless roar of the breakers was both deafening and irritating, fleas infested the mens' clothing and blankets, and the holiday menus were far from festive. The closest resemblance to bread was prepared with a meal ground from the bulb of the lilylike camass plant, and a root known as the "wappato" offered a tolerable substitute for potatoes. On Christmas Day, Clark lamented, "Our Diner concisted of pore Elk, so much Spoiled that we eate it thro mear necessity. Some pounded fish and a fiew roots."

The rainy winter lingered on until March of 1806 when the party broke camp and headed back east on an overland route that varied slightly from the way it had come. As the spring run of the salmon had not yet begun, the Indians along the Columbia River were living largely on mosses, lichens, and the inner bark of trees. Somehow the members of the expedition managed to stay alive until the most rigorous part of the journey was behind them and they were back in the country of the buffalo. But it was not until September, when they had almost reached their original jumping-off point of St. Louis on the Missouri River, that they again tasted the longed-for biscuit, pork, and whiskey that were then the staples of the American frontier.

Mountain Men & Oregon Homesteaders

THE NEWS OF THE LEWIS AND CLARK EX-plorations spread with astonishing speed. Hardly had the expedition returned when trappers and fur traders, learning that beaver were plentiful in the Rockies and sea otter on the Pacific coast, were headed for the wilds no matter what their hardships. This rough and fearless breed of lone wanderers, dedicating all their energies to the collection of pelts—particularly beaver, which was much in demand for men's hats—were known as mountain men.

A solitary year in the wilderness, seeking out the best beaver streams across a region that today embraces Colorado, Wyoming, Montana, Idaho, and Utah, was a readily accepted challenge for the daring throughout

the thirty years or so following the Lewis and Clark discoveries. If a mountain man had his leg chewed off by a grizzly bear, ran afoul of the local Indians, or was forced to eat snakemeat or some other "varmint" to survive, it was all part of the scheme whereby one might grow rich by exploiting nature, without having to be harnessed to a plow.

As to their victuals, the fur trappers of the Rockies were on a year-round camping trip. They carried with them sacks of coffee and sugar, flour and meal for baking biscuits and corncakes, and salt and pepper for seasoning the freshly shot meat that was their mainstay. In addition, they laid in supplies of whiskey and tobacco, creature comforts that were almost as vital as the powder and shot that earned the hunters their livelihood.

Once a year, groups of mountain men gathered at fixed rendezvous points in order to sell their furs and replenish their supplies. The green summer valley of Jackson Hole in Wyoming and the tranquil shores of Bear Lake on the Idaho-Utah border were favorite gathering places for the mountain trappers with their bundles of pelts and for the merchants and fur company agents who journeyed all the way from St. Louis. Indians also appeared at these meeting places with furs and hides to trade for blankets, cloth, knives, and other manufactured goods.

As supplies traveled west from Missouri, their price rose with every mile. If sugar was ten cents a pound in St. Louis, it cost a dollar a pound or more at the rendezvous site. The same was true of coffee, rifles, beaver traps, rum, or whatever else the mountain man required for his next winter's operations. Still, a skilled, energetic, and lucky hunter could turn a handy profit on the sale of his skins.

appeared once again on the shelves of the family larder.

Once homesteading got under way, the moist temperate valleys graced with summer sunshine proved splendid for the growing of cultivated varieties of fruits, berries, and nuts, as well as wheat and other staples. By 1847, trees and grafting stock were being brought overland from the central states for orchards of apples, pears, plums, prunes, cherries, filberts, and walnuts. In addition to the wild-growing blackberry, it was found that many cultivated varieties of raspberry, blueberry, strawberry, currant, and gooseberry flourished in the Pacific Northwest, while newly developed hybrids like the loganberry and the youngberry also throve.

The Oregon and Washington in which the Lewis and Clark Expedition had lived on dried fish and pounded roots, decaying elk meat, and slaughtered dogs turned out to be a garden of paradise for the provident new farmers. After a good wheat harvest, there was fine bread to eat and a marvelous dessert called summer pudding that was prepared by stewing wild or cultivated berries with sugar and then layering buttered slices of a delicate white loaf among the fruit. The contents of the pudding dish would then be firmly pressed down beneath a heavy weight so that the berry juices made the bread sweet and cakelike. At the same time the juices would stain the bread a rich berry color. Served cold with heavy cream, summer pudding was a dish that wiped out the memory of the lean and hungry times on the Oregon Trail. Somehow it helped make the harsh journey and the disasters that had befallen wagons, cattle, and members of families seem to have been not wholly in vain.

❧⊰⊱❧

On the Trail
of California Gold

"WHEN I WENT TO CALIFORNIA IN 1841
all the foreigners—and all were foreigners except Indians and Mexicans—did not, I think, exceed one hundred." So wrote John Bidwell, the leader of one of the
first overland parties to reach the "Golden State" at a
time when it was a sleepy string of Franciscan missions
and frontier ranches under the rule of Mexico. The
Americans he found in California were, according to
Bidwell, an unsavory lot of unkempt mountain men
"who would let their beards grow down to their knees,"
horse thieves "sometimes driving off four or five
hundred at a time," and sailors "who had run away from
vessels and remained in the country."

The pinpoints of civilization were the old Spanish missions stretching along the coast in a chain of twenty-one,
from San Diego in the south to Sonoma in the north.
The picturesque churches with their adobe outbuildings
were estimated to be a day's journey apart on a trail
known as El Camino Real, "the royal road." As in New
Mexico and throughout the Southwest, the padres shep-
herded the local Indians, guiding them into the Roman
Catholic faith and teaching them the cultivation of olives, grapes, citrus fruits, figs, pears, apricots, and pome-
granates, as well as wheat, on the mission farms.

The fertility of the California valleys had not been
probed by the Indians of the region prior to the arrival
of the Franciscan friars and the establishment of the

first mission in 1769. In California and Nevada, a rugged terrain composed of steep mountains and rocky desertlands separated the tribal groups into small clusters that engaged primarily in food-gathering rather than food-growing. Among the Maidu, Pomo, and Hupa of central and northern California, for example, acorns were the mainstay.

So much labor was involved in removing the acorn nut from its hard, woody sheath and in extracting the poisonous, bitter-tasting tannin from the acorn meal that one wonders if it might not have been less trouble to grow corn or beans. Yet the lives of the people had revolved for centuries around the processes of gathering acorns, crushing their shells to hull them, grinding them between stones to a fine meal, and then purifying the meal by spreading it out in a pit and repeatedly pouring hot water through it.

When sweet enough and safe to eat, the meal was baked into a bread or cooked to a porridge. It could also be stewed with rabbit, antelope, or other game. The California Indians were basket weavers rather than potters, so their cooking was done in tightly woven baskets by the stone-boiling method, which was practiced by nearly all the Pacific coast tribes. A cooking basket filled with water was placed in a shallow pit in the ground. Red-hot stones, heated in the fire, were then added to the water until it grew hot enough to boil. Of course, the cooled stones had to be removed and freshly heated ones added all the time, so the Indian woman often put in an entire day of pot-watching in order to serve up an evening dinner of boiled meat and acorn dumplings.

Among the Indians of the semidesert country of Nevada, starvation was an ever-present threat. The so-called "Digger" Indians lived largely by grubbing for roots and ate grasshoppers and other insects. In 1841, John Bidwell told of coming upon a group of Diggers, possibly Paiutes, near the Humboldt Sink, a depression into which Nevada's Humboldt River flowed and then evaporated. The Indians were gathering the sweet, sticky secretion of the tule plant, a type of bulrush that grew in the Humboldt marshes. Although the "honey" was covered with tiny crawling ants, it was scooped up "into balls about the size of one's fist," and eaten on the spot, for the clinging insects were a valuable source of nourishment too.

Upon reaching California, Bidwell and his party remained for a short time with an American rancher in the nearly uninhabited San Joaquin Valley. However, as their host soon set the Mexican authorities against them, he and his companions decided to head north toward the Sacramento Valley where a new colony was being founded by a Swiss immigrant named John Sutter.

Sutter's Fort embraced a variety of enterprises— wheat-farming, fur-trapping, lumbering, distilling, and cattle-ranching, mainly for the production of tallow and hides. Sutter had well over a hundred employees of various trades and backgrounds. And it was one of Sutter's men, a carpenter engaged in building a sawmill on the American River in January of 1848, who discovered a nugget of gold in the crystal clear water of the millrace.

Although communications were slow in the 1840s, the news traveled with uncanny speed. By 1849 the gold rush was on, with people scrambling to get to California by any route or means available. Some traveled overland, starting out on the Santa Fe Trail or branching off from the Oregon Trail; others made their way by boat. The longer but surer route was via Cape Horn at the tip of South America, while a shorter journey was by ship from the East coast to Panama, then across the isthmus on foot or muleback, and finally up the West coast by ship to California.

Swindles and cruel tricks were played on the gold-hungry Easterners. Many crossed the steaming jungles of Panama, becoming racked with fever and dysentery, only to find themselves stranded. Although California had become a possession of the United States at the close of the Mexican War in 1848, the gold-seekers came from all over the world, many arriving at Pacific ports on foreign vessels that were often deserted by their crews and sometimes even by their officers.

Almost overnight the primeval wilderness of California was transformed into a roaring scene. Prospectors were everywhere, tearing up the hillsides, diverting and muddying the streams, as they wielded pickaxes and shovels, tossing dirt and rocks in all directions in their feverish search for gold. At first, placer mining—washing, or panning, for gold particles in stream beds—yielded gold dust and even large nuggets. But as the streams became worked over, the miners began their search for the mother veins that lay deep in the mountains.

All this time the cost of food, clothing, blankets, tools, and other mining supplies was skyrocketing. Towns with names like Red-Dog, You-Bet, Ground Hog Glory, and Old Dry Diggins did a land-office business in outfitting the goldseekers and providing recreation in the form of gambling houses that were also drinking establishments and dance halls. Thievery and even murder were not uncommon, and Old Dry Diggins soon became known as Hangtown because of the number of criminals that received swift justice there by hanging.

Like most mining towns during the gold rush, Hangtown "consisted of one long straggling street of clapboard houses and log cabins." As further described by a visiting Scotsman, J. D. Bothwick, in 1851, "The street itself was in many places knee-deep in mud, and was plentifully strewed with old boots, hats, and shirts, old sardine boxes, worn out pots and kettles, old hambones, broken picks and shovels, and other rubbish too various to particularise."

But the prices of Hangtown's eateries were hardly in keeping with the squalor without. Hungry miners paid lavishly in gold for a meal known as the Hangtown fry—a mess of fried eggs, fried oysters, and bacon. Since eggs alone sold for fifty cents each in the general store, bread and onions went for a dollar a pound, and bacon and oysters were practically worth their weight in gold, such a meal, cooked and served, might easily run six or seven dollars. It is not surprising that the Hangtown fry became a status symbol for those prospectors who had struck it rich.

Off in the hills where the mining camps were located, prices were even more inflated. In his *Six Months in the Gold Fields,* published in 1850, Edward Gould Buffum reported paying forty-three dollars for breakfast victuals for two! The provisions consisted of "one box of sardines, one pound of sea-biscuit, one pound of butter, a half-pound of cheese, and two bottles of ale." The profiteering and general notoriety of some of the campsites and mining towns became so great that after a time many changed their names. Hangtown took back one of its earlier names of Placerville, after the placer-mining creek beside which it had been built, and grew into a settled, stable community

⬳⧉⬱

The Chinese
in San Francisco

AMONG THE GOLD-SEEKERS WHO SWARMED into California in the late 1840s and early 1850s, about three-fourths were not American-born. They included Europeans from Great Britain, France, and Germany; Peruvians and Chileans from South America; Mexicans from south of the border; and from across the Pacific, Australians, Hawaiians, and Chinese.

Most of the Chinese newcomers were peasants, dreaming of a single lucky gold strike with which to return to their homes in the Celestial Empire, pay off their debts, and perhaps even become as wealthy as the landowners under whose oppression most of them lived. Few, of course, struck it rich, and as early as 1852, the Chinese found themselves discriminated against in the mining camps. Their wages were lower than those of the white miners—as little as seventy-five cents a day—and they were required to pay a head tax as high as four dollars a month for laboring in the gold fields. Still, the influx of Oriental immigrants continued, and as the months and years passed, mining opportunities gave way to other means of earning a livelihood in the rapidly growing port city of San Francisco and its surroundings.

Many Chinese became domestic servants in the homes of the new business elite and the wealthy ranchers of the area. Others found jobs as cooks in mining camps, lumber camps, and later in railroad camps. Some under-

took truck gardening on small patches of land, growing bean sprouts and bamboo shoots, snow peas and water chestnuts—the delicate-flavored, crunchy, and succulent vegetables that were used in their traditional dishes.

Beginning in 1864, Asian immigration leaped even higher as thousands of unskilled laborers called coolies were brought from the teeming cities of southern China to the West coast to build the Central Pacific Railroad. The rail line crept eastward from Sacramento to a point in Utah where, five years later, it met the Union Pacific Railroad, which had been constructed westward from Omaha.

The Irish, German, and Scandinavian immigrant laborers of the Union Pacific suffered the attacks of angrily aroused Indian hunters of the Great Plains and stampeding buffalo, and they had to scale the passes of the Rockies. But the terrain crossed by the Central Pacific was even more treacherous. Untold numbers of Chinese workers lost their lives grading the roadbed over the Sierra Nevadas, building bridges across deep gorges and lashing rivers, blasting and hacking their way through solid rock to create rail tunnels, and finally struggling across the harsh Nevada desertlands. The ceremonial driving in of the final golden spike in 1869 signalled the start of a new travel era, one in which the entire American continent could be crossed for the first time by rail.

The Chinese were credited little, if at all, for their sacrifice toward this achievement. If anything, their much-increased population was held in greater contempt than ever. "I cannot find terms severe enough with which to censure the conduct of the Californians toward the Chinese," wrote Baron von Hübner, an Austrian diplomat who visited America in 1871. "Without the least provocation, the Chinese are constantly beaten and robbed." The only crime of these patient toilers, von Hübner observed, appeared to be their acceptance of the low wages paid them by their white employers, thus crowding non-Orientals out of the labor market and earning the Chinese the ugly epithet of "the Yellow Peril." Once the economic slump of the 1870s gripped the nation, public hostility toward the Chinese in California flared to a fever pitch, culminating in the Oriental Exclusion Acts of the 1880s, which prohibited Asians from entering the United States.

By that time, however, San Francisco's Chinatown had come into existence as a close-knit, self-protective community in which Chinese culture with its artisans, food markets, and family traditions flourished. Although the hired Chinese servants of white Californians did not always "cook Chinese" for their employers, the ancient approach to cookery was carefully followed in the Chinese quarters.

Based on the principal of rapid cooking because of a limited supply of fuel, all meats and vegetables were finely cut, sliced, or diced into uniform sizes before being placed over the fire. According to the methods of Canton, the southern port city and its surrounding province from which so many Chinese immigrants had come, the ingredients were then quickly sautéed in a small amount of oil by a process known as stir-frying. This gave the vegetables, which predominated in most dishes, a wonderfully crisp, fresh flavor, very different from the soggy taste and limp appearance of the customarily overcooked and waterlogged American vegetables. The usual cooking vessel was the *wok,* a large, bowl-like, round-bottomed pan that rested on a rim on the surface of a Chinese stove, extending part way into the fire-hole.

In nineteenth-century America, Chinese cooking was

regarded as a curiosity, rarely appreciated for its delicate and subtle flavors, its thrifty use of fuel and meat, or its healthful preservation of food nutrients. However, Chinese recipes for beef, pork, or poultry, with a selection of appropriate vegetables (often in the proportion suggested by Confucius of one-fourth meat and three-fourths vegetables) have shown us how foods can be successfully cooked in their own juices without the addition of water or other liquids and how varied and tantalizing in texture and flavor such dishes can be. Even the accompanying rice, the grain most popular throughout the southern half of China, is cooked in only as much water as is required to be absorbed for tenderness. No nutritious cooking liquids need ever be poured down the kitchen sink.

It is perhaps only in the latter half of the twentieth century—well over a hundred years since the gold rush brought the first Chinese to America—that the contributions, both culinary and otherwise, of this remarkable people are at last being fully recognized.

Mediterranean Gardeners in Southern California

WHILE THE GOLD COAST OF NORTHERN California rang with the sounds of barroom brawls and mining excavations, the southern half of the state was still, in 1850, a quiet backwater. Its largest town, the

Pueblo de los Angeles, was a center of Mexican-flavored ranch life. The surrounding bays and hills were full of waterfowl and quail, deer, antelope, and elk, while the peaceful valleys grew some grapes and orchard fruits. The author of *Six Months in the Gold Fields,* on a visit to Los Angeles, wrote, "The country around the Pueblo is by far the most favorable portion of southern California for the settlement of foreigners. Possessing a climate of unequaled mildness and a soil of great fertility, it must inevitably, ere long, be surrounded by a large population."

Yet it was not until after the completion of the transcontinental railroad that the village of Los Angeles, which was first visited in 1826 by the mountain man, Jedediah Smith, grew from a population of a few thousand to over 50,000 and, by 1900, had passed the 100,000 mark. Due to the competition between two privately owned branch railways, the fare for the entire trip from Kansas City to Los Angeles plunged at one point to one dollar! This occurred during the 1880s, a period when immigration to the United States from southern and eastern Europe was mounting rapidly.

As the original Spanish settlers of southern California had discovered, the region strongly resembled Mediterranean Europe. The climate was warm and somewhat dry, with rain occurring mainly in the winter. Although summer irrigation was necessary for some crops, the sun was dependable as was the freedom from killing frosts. Italian, Greek, and Portuguese farmers, among others, were strongly attracted to the southern half of California in the last two decades of the nineteenth century. Once settled there, they undertook the cultivation of numerous kinds of fruits and vegetables, transforming the area into a produce market that would, in time, serve the growing nation.

The valleys of the central part of the state became vineyards, growing wine grapes as well as table and raisin grapes, while the extreme south put in additional orchards of semitropical and tropical fruits, including limes, grapefruits, citrons, guavas, mangoes, and papayas, as well as dates, figs, prunes, apricots, and English walnuts. From this bounty and variety were to come a special category of "California" desserts to enliven the culinary scene. Among them were such fruit creations as date torte and prune whip, grapefruit pie and guava marmalade, and all sorts of breads, muffins, cakes, and cookies generously studded with California's dried fruits and nuts.

Truck gardens sprang up everywhere in California, and in these the immigrant growers could express their preferences of well-loved greens and other vegetables from the Old World. Broccoli, an Italian relative of the cauliflower, zucchini, an Italian squash, and artichokes, a favorite throughout southern Europe, were among the vegetables grown in California in the 1880s and 1890s that later became popular throughout the United States.

In preparing their traditional vegetable dishes, the Mediterranean peoples on the Pacific used ingredients like olive oil, pungent hard cheese, plenty of garlic and black pepper, and herbs like basil and oregano, which they also introduced to their American neighbors. Yet instead of blending into the "melting pot," the name given to the cultural ferment of turn-of-the-century America, the dishes of each ethnic group seemed to retain their identity in their new setting.

Fortunately, this trend has continued. Rather than mingling into a characterless blend, the cuisines of the nation's immigrants have, for the most part, held their own and thereby enriched the culinary scene for everyone.

Recipes from

the Far West

◆§ SUMMER PUDDING

  2   cups fresh blueberries, blackberries, or raspberries (1 pint)

  ½   cup sugar

  ¼   teaspoon cinnamon

  6   slices white bread (rich, crumbly type)
      sweet butter, softened
      heavy cream or whipped cream

Pick over and wash berries; drain, and put into a medium-size saucepan. Add sugar, cinnamon, and 2 tablespoons water. Heat, stirring, until mixture becomes juicy and bubbly. Simmer about 5 minutes.

Lightly butter bottom and sides of a one-quart casserole or deep pudding dish. Trim crusts from bread slices and butter slices well. Cut each into four quarters. Line bottom of dish with one-third of the bread pieces, almost touching. Spoon over one-third of the hot berry mixture. Repeat twice, using up all the bread and the stewed berries.

Cover pudding with an inverted plate, pressed down hard. A heavy object such as a large jar of jam may be placed atop the plate. Chill in refrigerator several hours.

Serve summer pudding with heavy cream or lightly sweetened whipped cream atop each portion. Serves 5–6.

✎ *GINGER CHICKEN WITH SNOW PEAS*

2   cups boneless and skinless raw chicken breast, cut in ½-inch cubes (about 1½ pounds before skinning and boning)

2   tablespoons soy sauce

3   tablespoons dry vermouth or dry sherry

4   teaspoons cornstarch
peanut oil (about 5 tablespoons)
salt

1   medium-size sweet red pepper (or green pepper) cut in ½-inch squares

6   scallions (green onions), cut in ¼-inch cross-slices

1   clove garlic, put through garlic press

3   dime-size slices fresh ginger, cut in tiny pieces

1   cup fresh snow peas (or one 6-ounce package frozen snow peas, slightly thawed)

½   pound fresh mushrooms, washed and cut in ½-inch cubes

2   tablespoons strong chicken broth (you may use instant broth powder plus water)

1   teaspoon sesame oil

Combine soy sauce, vermouth or sherry, and cornstarch. Divide mixture in half. Combine first half in a shallow bowl with cut-up chicken, cover tightly with plastic wrap, and marinate several hours in refrigerator. Set rest of sauce mixture aside.

Cut up all ingredients as indicated. Start cooking

about one-half hour before serving time. Heat a Chinese wok or a steep-sided, heavy, 10-inch skillet on range until very hot. Add about 2 tablespoons of the peanut oil. Add red or green pepper squares and the white parts of the scallions. Add garlic and ginger. Sprinkle all lightly with salt, and stir-fry, for 5–7 minutes, by moving vegetables around in pan with a long wooden spoon until just approaching tenderness but still crisp. With a slotted spoon, remove contents to a heated bowl.

Add 1 more tablespoon of peanut oil to hot wok. Add snow peas, whole, and the green parts of the scallions. Salt lightly and stir-fry 3–4 minutes. Remove to heated bowl.

Add 1 more tablespoon oil. Add mushrooms and re-peat as above. After removing mushrooms, allow any liquid in wok to evaporate over high heat. Add a final tablespoon of oil and the chicken pieces with their marinade. Cook, stirring, until chicken loses its pink color. Return all vegetables from heated bowl to wok and mix through very gently.

Add chicken broth and sesame oil to remaining half of soy sauce mixture and blend well. Add to contents of wok and cook a few minutes, just until sauce is clear and starchy taste has disappeared. Transfer contents of wok to heated bowl and serve at once. If allowed to stand any length of time, vegetables will lose their crispness and go limp.

The only accompaniment necessary is boiled white rice. Just before starting to cook ginger chicken, combine ¾ cup raw rice, washed and well drained, 1½ cups water, and 1 teaspoon salt in a medium-size saucepan. Cover, bring to boil, reduce heat, and let rice cook on very low heat until grains are tender and all water is absorbed. This recipe for ginger chicken with snow peas, plus rice, serves 4.

⋘ DATE AND WALNUT BARS

½ cup butter or margarine (¼ pound or 1 stick), softened at room temperature
¾ cup dark brown sugar, firmly packed
2 eggs
1½ cups cut-up pitted dates
½ cup golden raisins
1 cup coarsely chopped walnuts
2 tablespoons grated orange rind
1 tablespoon orange juice
⅔ cup sifted all-purpose flour
1 teaspoon baking powder

Preheat oven to 350 degrees Fahrenheit.

Put butter or margarine in a medium-large mixing bowl and mash it with the back of a wooden spoon until creamy. Add sugar and continue creaming until well blended. Add eggs, one at a time, and beat well with a wire whisk.

To cut dates, use a scissors dipped in cold water. Cut each date into three or four pieces. Add dates, raisins, walnuts, orange rind, and orange juice to creamed mixture. Combine flour and baking powder and sift into mixture. Stir only until blended.

Turn batter into a well-greased 9 × 9 × 2 or 8 × 8 × 2 baking pan. Bake 35 minutes or until top of cake springs back when lightly pressed with finger and edges have come away slightly from sides of pan. Cool on wire rack, with a linen or cotton towel covering top of pan to keep contents moist.

When thoroughly cool, cut cake with sharp knife slicing it into eight strips about an inch wide and then crosswise into three sections about three inches long. Store in tightly-covered tin. Makes 24 date and walnut bars.

⋘ ZUCCHINI PARMESAN

2   pounds zucchini, medium-large
    butter or margarine
    olive oil or salad oil
    salt, black pepper, dried basil, dried oregano
1   large clove garlic, put through garlic press
2   tablespoons freshly grated parmesan or romano
      cheese
1   tablespoon dried bread crumbs

Pare zucchini with potato peeler, slice off ends, wash, and slice into disks one-eighth inch thick. Place 1 tablespoon butter or margarine and 1 tablespoon olive or salad oil in a 10-inch skillet, and heat to sizzling.

Arrange one layer of zucchini slices in skillet, sprinkle very lightly with salt, pepper, basil, and oregano. Sprinkle with about one-quarter of the pressed garlic clove. When slices are transparent and very lightly browned, turn and sauté other side. Remove zucchini to a lightly buttered one-quart oven casserole. Add a little more fat and oil to skillet and a second layer of zucchini. Add seasonings as before, sauté on both sides, and add to casserole. Continue until all zucchini slices are used. Set oven to 350 degrees Fahrenheit.

Combine cheese and bread crumbs. After half the zucchini slices are in the casserole dish, sprinkle with half the cheese and crumb mixture. Repeat with second half. Dot top with butter or margarine and bake, uncovered, for 20 minutes. Serve from baking dish. Zucchini parmesan is especially good with baked or broiled chicken. Serves 4–5.

Pioneers in the
Cities Back East

AT THE SAME TIME AMERICA'S
frontiers were being expanded westward across the
wilderness, pioneers were also hewing out new patterns
of life in the nation's cities—both the older cities of the
Eastern seaboard and the younger ones that were closely
following the advancing frontier. These pioneers of the
cities were part of the growing trend toward urban living, the very note on which the nineteenth century was
to close.

In 1800 only one out of every twenty Americans lived
in a town or city; in 1900 one out of every three did.
Some of the cities that sprang to life during the 1800s—
Cincinnati, Chicago, New Orleans, Detroit, St. Louis,
Minneapolis, San Francisco, Los Angeles—grew into
thriving metropolises within thirty years or less. Their
populations were swelled by rural people drifting to
places of greater opportunity and by immigrant groups
that clustered in urban centers. The fledgling giants
varied in character but tended, nevertheless, to model
themselves on the older cities of the East coast, which
would always be venerable and awe-inspiring symbols of
colonial America.

During the century of pioneer America, the colonial

cities did not remain static. Philadelphia, which had
been one of the largest centers of population in the British Empire, came to outrank Berlin, Germany, by the
mid-1800s, and New York, by 1900, was more populous
than Paris. The flavors of the colonial cities also changed
drastically during the nineteenth century. Boston and
New York, major Atlantic ports, were much altered by
the immigrants who gravitated to them. The century of
pioneer America also witnessed the birth of a brand new
Eastern city, Washington, D.C., which underwent the
unique experience of finding out how to be the national
capital of the United States of America.

❧

French Elegance in the Jefferson White House

THOMAS JEFFERSON WAS THE FIRST PRESI-
dent to serve a full term in the nation's new capital. Its
core of official buildings, which had been completed in
1800, lay atop a swampy plain beside the Potomac River.
The site, once occupied by the Powhatan Indians, an
Algonquian tribe of the Eastern woodlands, had been
carefully selected to deal diplomatically with the issue of
slavery. Northern abolitionists objected to having the
seat of government in a slaveholding state, so the
Congress created the District of Columbia by carving
out a piece of territory that had once belonged to Maryland.

Among Washington, D.C.'s nearest neighbors were the Virginia plantation estates of George Washington (after whom the city was named) and other founding fathers, including Jefferson himself. Having been Minister to France from 1785 to 1789, the country's third president had been strongly influenced by French culture. He was particularly impressed with French *haute cuisine,* which was a far cry from the country-cured ham, grits and hominy, turnip and collard greens, fried apples, beaten biscuits and similar hotbreads that were customarily prepared by the slave kitchen staff of his Monticello home.

While in France, Jefferson took careful culinary notes, and many of the recipes that he brought back with him were later to grace the dinner tables at the White House as well as those at Monticello. His preferences set a pattern for elegance and refinement in dining that future presidents and their wives would follow. Jefferson introduced, via his French-trained cooks, a whole roster of sauces ranging from delicate cream sauces for fish or chicken to robust red wine sauces for meat and game. He saw to the cultivation of subtly flavored vegetables like artichokes, asparagus, mushrooms, and endive to replace the strong-flavored greens and starchy peas and beans of the American table.

The dessert delicacies he transplanted from France were marvels of airiness and richness. They included small cakes like macaroons and lady fingers, an almond-flavored milk pudding that went by the name of blancmange, a vanilla-flavored egg-and-cream custard known as *pots de crème,* and baked confections of beaten egg white and sugar called meringues. Jefferson gave his pastry cooks directions for baking the meringues in the shape of tart shells so that they could be filled with ice cream.

Long known in France and even earlier in Renaissance Italy, ice cream became the most popular White House dessert during Jefferson's two terms and also during that of James Madison, who followed him. As Jefferson was a widower when he came to office, Dolley Madison (whose husband was then Secretary of State) frequently acted as White House hostess. After she became first lady, Mrs. Madison's dinners and balls grew famous, and Washington wives took extraordinary pains to follow the lead of this stylish and vivacious hostess. Even at morning receptions, wine, punch, and cakes were served. A favorite of "Queen Dolley's" was seed cake, made from a rich buttery recipe that included caraway seeds and brandy.

The glitter of early Washington life was dimmed somewhat by the War of 1812. In August of 1814, just before British troops burned the White House, their officers came upon a dinner table handsomely laid for forty guests, with cut-glass decanters of wine cooling on the sideboard and spits of meat and brimming saucepans in the kitchen. Only hours earlier, the renowned hostess herself had fled the presidential mansion. After sitting down gleefully to the feast before them, one of the British officers wrote that he and his fellows "finished by setting fire to the house which had so liberally entertained them."

By 1818 the White House had been rebuilt and Washington society was back to normal. At a "small" dinner party for twelve given by a Washington hostess in 1835, the soup and fish courses were followed by canvasback duck, pheasant, ham, turkey, partridge, mutton chops, and sweetbreads. This overabundance of meat dishes was typical of the groaning dinner tables of the day. But, in deference to the genteel influence of Thomas Jefferson, the rich pies and heavy plum puddings that most Americans would have consumed for dessert did not appear. Instead the hostess produced an array of the more fashionable ice creams, fruits, custards, and blancmange. Since Jefferson's day, even nuts, figs, and raisins were considered too vulgar to grace a table in the nation's capital.

As the country expanded, backwoods Congressmen arriving in Washington were stunned and indignant at what they viewed as the culinary extravagances of the White House. In 1840, one member of the House of Representatives delivered a lengthy tirade against the presidential "palace," where dishes like hog and hominy, fried meat and gravy, and hard cider were too old-fashioned and commonplace for the "Court banqueting room." Table furnishings there consisted of "massive gold plate and French sterling silver services, blue and gold French tambours, compotiers on feet, stands for bonbons, with three stages, gilded French plateaus, garnished with mirrors and garlands, and gaudy artificial flowers."

Indeed, the French influences on the Washington scene were criticized many times during the capital's first half-century. The city itself had been designed by a French engineer, Pierre L'Enfant, and among its early residents had been affluent French emigrés who had fled the French Revolution during the 1790s. As the national attitude toward Great Britain had been so bitter following the American Revolution, it was hardly surprising that the manners and customs of the new American capital should have been modeled on those of the French rather than the British.

By the time of the Civil War, native American traditions had begun to assert themselves more and more strongly in Washington. The custom of chewing tobacco was carried onto Capitol Hill and directly into the Capitol building where the carpets of both houses of Congress were hideously stained with tobacco juice. Charles Dickens wrote in his *American Notes* of the "universal disregard of the spittoon" in the Senate, where "an honorable gentleman leaning back in his tilted chair, with his legs on the desk before him" would cut a fresh plug of tobacco with his penknife and, just before placing it in his cheek, could be seen "shooting the old one from his mouth as from a pop-gun." Dickens observed that "even steady old chewers of great experience are not always good marksmen."

The Senators also expressed their down-home food preferences in a dish that was to become a regular offering in the Senate restaurant: U.S. Senate bean soup, prepared with traditional early American ingredients—dried white pea beans, onions, and a good-size ham bone with some meat clinging to it.

In the long run, both elements in Washington, D.C. had their way. The tobacco-spitting lawmakers continued to enjoy the steaming lunchtime bowls of hearty bean soup that appeared daily on the Senate menu, while the White House went on overfeeding its guests in the fashion of the day, but with distinct touches of deference to Jeffersonian elegance.

At the wedding breakfast given by President Ulysses S. Grant for his daughter Nellie in May of 1874, the menu consisted of soft-shell crabs, chicken croquettes, lamb cutlets, beef tongue in aspic, woodcock, and snipe. The morning repast ended with strawberries in cream followed by charlotte russe, Nesselrode pudding, blancmange, ice cream, water ices, small fancy cakes, and wedding cake, to say nothing of punch and champagne.

✢✤✢

Boston: Refuge from the Potato Famine

". . . Boston,
The home of the bean and the cod,
Where the Lowells talk only to Cabots
And the Cabots talk only to God."

SO AMERICA'S HISTORIC CITY, FOUNDED in 1630, was toasted at a college alumni dinner in 1910. Yet, turn-of-the-century Boston was no longer the austere, almost snobbish city of the descendants of English Puritan families, such as the Cabots and the Lowells, which had produced generations of educators, religious leaders, writers, scientists, and prosperous New England manufacturers and businessmen.

As early as the 1840s, the society surrounding the high-caste "Boston Brahmins" and their fellow-citizens of British ancestry was beginning to change radically. Across the sea, in Ireland, the potato crop had failed, and starvation was sending streams of emigrants to the New World.

Boston seemed a natural destination. Irish and Scotch-Irish settlers had been entering through its port since colonial times, with many going on to pioneer in the Ohio and Kentucky country. Most of those immigrants had been of the Protestant faith.

The new wave were mainly Catholics. For generations they had lived on small farms or worked as tenant-farmers on British-owned estates in Ireland. Before the introduction of the white potato from South America, their principal food had been the parsnip, supplemented with other root vegetables, cabbage, oatmeal porridge, and occasional mutton or game. But once the potato was taken up as a staple food, the Irish enthusiastically made it their very own. Hence, when Irish settlers first planted the potato in New Hampshire in 1719, it was immediately accepted as the "Irish potato," despite its origin in Peru.

The blight that destroyed the Irish potato crop in 1845 and the years following brought widespread suffering. By 1847, 750,000 Irish had died of hunger and over 200,000 had fled to the United States. Opportunities existed for work on canals and railroads, in mines and in the building trades, and the newcomers took these jobs rather than seek out new farms, as had their countrymen who arrived a century earlier. Large numbers of Irish remained in Boston, while somewhat smaller groups clustered in Chicago and other cities. Urban living was more congenial to the Irish Catholics because churches of their faith were virtually nonexistent in the smaller towns and in the countryside of Protestant America. As the famine years wore on, more and more immigrants joined their kin in America, and Boston became an Irish-flavored city. All in all, about two million Irish entered the United States between 1830 and 1860, most of them in the years following the onset of the potato famine.

City living, a new experience for the immigrants as well as for most Americans in the 1840s, brought its own problems. Within a few years of the arrival of the first heavy waves of newcomers, Boston's poorer neighborhoods had become overcrowded and squalid. The sanitation, health care, police and fire-fighting facilities of the city were totally inadequate to deal with such heavy concentrations of people, and human miseries, aside from hunger, were rampant. Although jobs were available for the unskilled in mills and factories, as clerks and errand boys, as scrubwomen and washer-women, the hours were long, the pay was minimal, and sweatshop conditions prevailed. Among those who were more successful at making their way in the New World, many found places in public service and in political or-ganizations, some of which became political machines for the manipulation of Boston's large Irish Catholic vote. Despite corrupt practices, the ward bosses were also benefactors of the immigrant population, and by 1900 the descendants of Irish immigrants were domi-nating the Boston political scene.

Despite the severe prejudice the potato-famine Irish first encountered in the New World, largely because of their Catholic religion, these pioneers of the city man-aged not only to survive but to extend their influence over the established population. Irish cuisine, although not extensive, began to spread itself across the Boston that had long been known as Beantown. This name derived from the Puritan custom of slow-baking beans on Saturday, the busy, chore-filled day before the Sun-day Sabbath. On Saturday evening, the contents of the fragrant beanpot, simmering in juices flavored with onion, salt pork, and molasses, were ladled out and eaten with Boston brown bread and pickles. The left-over beans were kept warm overnight in the fireplace oven to be eaten again on Sunday morning before the family took off for the lengthy church service.

The Irish immigrants of the nineteenth century wholeheartedly adopted such early New England dishes as boiled corned beef and cabbage, with plenty of pota-toes of course, and also the entire range of New En-gland chowders and fish stews: clam, codfish, sea bass,

been renamed Castle Garden and converted into a reception and clearing center for the city's newcomers from abroad. Its facilities, however, were limited and hardly prepared to cope with the unforeseen swell of immigration that was to hit the city with stunning impact in the years between 1882 and 1900.

Not a crop failure this time but the assassination of a foreign monarch was to spur the flight of hundreds of thousands to the United States. In 1881 in Russia, the moderately liberal Czar Alexander II had been murdered by terrorists. Long subjected to numerous restrictions and frequent persecutions, the five million Jews who lived in Russia once more became the targets of the organized massacres known as pogroms under the new czar, the despotic Alexander III.

Even in the tiny, scattered Jewish villages, with their mud streets and ramshackle houses, the wretched inhabitants had heard something of the late-nineteenth-century America to which many Europeans had already emigrated. Yet, few of those emigrants, so far, had been Jews. In the entire United States in 1881, there were only about 250,000 Jews. Most were of German origin, although several thousand Dutch, Spanish, and Portuguese Jews had settled in America before and during the Revolutionary period. Widely distributed around the country, many had been assimilated into non-Jewish communities and had abandoned their religion and traditions.

The Jews that now poured out of Russia and other parts of eastern Europe were a new and different immigrant group for the United States. Their traditions were those of the *shtetl,* the ghettolike Jewish village or small town in which most had lived. As Jews were generally not permitted to own land in Russia, few were farmers. They had survived by working as tailors, cobblers, carpenters, or other kinds of artisans, by trading, and often simply by their wits. Many, supported by their families or the community, had devoted their entire lives to religious scholarship.

Like the potato-famine Irish in Boston, the new arrivals tended to cluster in the city, bound together by their religion, their strong family ties, and their language, Yiddish, which was based on old German dialects and had become enriched over the years with borrowings from other European tongues. As a rapidly-growing manufacturing center, the city of New York offered the immigrants some of the kinds of skilled work for which they were qualified, especially in the needle and fur trades. Many of those who were unskilled became street peddlers or small merchants.

The city's lower East Side, the center of immigrant Jewish life, soon thronged with humanity, living in crowded, dingy, and unsanitary tenements. The streets, too, were frantically congested with horse-drawn wagons, pushcarts, vendors calling their wares, haggling customers, children prancing and shouting at their games. Bewildered new arrivals just released from Castle Garden or Ellis Island (the new immigrant center opened in 1892), wandered through the neighborhood seeking out the addresses of relatives or friends. In the factories, shops, and home workshops, people bent over their tasks, often for twelve to fourteen hours a day, stumbling exhausted into their beds where sleeping frequently had to be arranged in shifts.

Like the Irish of Boston in the 1840s, these Jewish city pioneers of the 1880s and 1890s were often looked upon with fear and contempt. Americans of older stock saw them as "alien hordes" that were turning the United States into a "dumping ground" for foreign nations, threatening to despoil the character of the country. As

the closing decades of the century were plagued with re-
curring business depressions, the Jewish immigrants
were also regarded (like the California Chinese following the gold rush years) as unfair labor competition. Yet
out of the ferment and suffering of the Jewish immigrant experience came many rich contributions in the
fields of business and law, the sciences, the arts, and in-
tellectual life that were to benefit the entire nation in the
century that followed.

Not the least of the eastern European Jewish traditions that were to enrich New York City, and later the
national scene, was the kosher cuisine of this new seg-
ment of the population. Jewish foods and cookery were
based on a set of Hebrew dietary laws delivered to the
Jews by Moses over three thousand years earlier. They
were directed at stamping out ancient practices such as
animal sacrifices and the drinking of animal blood, at
avoiding unsanitary animal foods, and at swift and mer-
ciful killing of those animals slaughtered for food. From
the Mosaic law stating, "Thou shalt not seethe a kid in
its mother's milk," came the prohibition against mixing
dairy foods and meat products at the same meal. Pork
and pork products, shrimp, oysters, and other seafood
were forbidden to Jews because hogs and shellfish were
scavengers that devoured rotting vegetable and animal
matter. Other animal foods, such as beef, lamb, and
poultry, were permitted only if slaughtered according to
Hebrew ritual law and properly washed, salted, and
soaked to remove all traces of fresh blood.

Out of the "don'ts" of kosher cuisine came a whole
roster of foods that *could* be eaten and were raised to a
level of excellence. Among these were the Friday night
Sabboth loaf, or *challah,* a braided and twisted, golden-
brown, glazed bread of egg-rich yeast dough. The loaf

was formally blessed just before the family, no matter how poor, sat down to the scrubbed table covered with its white Sabbath cloth and glowing candles. Next at the Sabbath meal might come an appetizer of chopped liver or *gefilte* fish, tender balls of chopped or ground fish combined with onions, eggs, bread crumbs, and seasonings simmered in a fish stock and served cold with carrot slices, a bit of jellied broth, and sharp, tangy horseradish. Chicken soup of pale, trembling gold, with noodes or *matzoth*-ball dumplings floating in it would follow; then boiled or roasted chicken; and for dessert a compote of stewed dried fruits, spongecake or cookies made without butter or other dairy products, and glasses of steaming tea.

Elements of this, the classic Friday-night repast of the eastern European immigrant Jews, began to crop up in nonkosher and non-Jewish cookery in the New World. Other traditional Jewish foods, most of which had their origin in Russian cookery, became popular snacks. Among these were the doughnut-shaped bagel, smeared with cream cheese and topped with glistening pink slices of smoked salmon, popularly known as "lox," and the baked, pastrylike *knish,* enclosing a center of well-seasoned mashed potato or *kasha,* the cooked buckwheat-groats cereal of Russia.

Many of the Jewish foods were closely associated with the holy days of the Hebrew calendar year. *Matzoth,* the large, flat, crackerlike wafers of Passover, commemorated the hasty departure of the Jews from Egypt at the time of the Exodus, in the 1200s B.C. To make good their escape from their oppressors, the Jews had to bake their bread before it had time to rise. These "unleavened loaves" are still eaten for the entire eight days of the Passover holiday in early spring, during which time the traditionalist Jew touches no leavened bread.

Dairy dishes like cheese-filled *blintzes,* delicate crepes that resemble the Russian *blinchiki,* are eaten at the holiday of Shevuoth which falls in May or June. According to legend, the Jews waited so long on this day at the foot of Mount Sinai for the Ten Commandments that all the fresh milk in their tents soured and had to be made into cheese. *Kreplach,* pockets of noodle dough filled with cottage cheese, are also popular at Shevuoth. A cousin to the Chinese *won ton* and the Italian ravioli, kreplach may also be prepared with a meat or chicken filling for other holiday meals.

Honey is the symbolic food for Rosh Hashonah, the Jewish New Year, which arrives in September or early October. This is a period of stock-taking, of quiet joy, and of hope that the future will be tinged with sweetness. Honey is baked into the nut-studded, spicy-brown *lekach,* the traditional honey cake and, at the New Year meal, it is the custom to eat slices of apple dipped into honey.

Rosh Hashonah is closely followed by Yom Kippur, the solemn Day of Atonement, a time of fasting and prayers. No food or water are taken from sundown on the previous day until after sundown on the day of Yom Kippur. The final meal must be free of salty or spicy foods, and the fast-breaking meal must not be too heavy or rich.

Sukkoth, in late September or in October, is the Hebrew harvest festival, a counterpart of America's Thanksgiving. In Europe, it was customary for the Jews to build leafy-bowered outdoor huts in which they ate their meals during this holiday. The huts commemorated the frail shelters in which the Jews lived during their flight from Egypt to Palestine. For the immigrant

Jews of New York's lower East Side, the rickety metal tenement-house fire escapes, decorated with leaves and branches, vegetables and fruits, served as substitutes for the traditional *sukkahs,* or huts. Eastern European Jews, at this holiday, ate *holishkes,* cabbage rolls stuffed with meat, and *strudel,* a pastry filled with apples or nuts.

Hanukkah, with its eight-day candle-lighting ceremony, usually arrives close to the time of Christmas and recalls the rededication of the Hebrew temple in Jerusalem after the defeat of the Syrians in 165 B.C. From a tiny jar of oil, the Jews miraculously managed to relight the holy lamps, one more each day until all eight were glowing. The most popular food for Hanukkah is *latkes,* crisp-edged potato pancakes, almost exactly like the German *Kartoffelpuffer.* But before the potato was introduced to eastern Europe, the holiday pancakes were made with buckwheat flour, a staple in Russia.

The holiday year rounds itself out with Purim in March, the happiest of all Jewish celebrations. It is also called the Feast of Esther because this Jewish wife of the king of Persia prevented the planned extermination of the Jews by the king's wicked councillor, Haman. *Nahit,* boiled and salted chick peas, are eaten at Purim, along with apples, nuts, and raisins, as a remembrance of Queen Esther's vegetarian diet at the Persian court, where kosher meats were not available.

The best known of Purim treats, however, are the little three-cornered cakes, usually filled with prune butter or poppy seeds, that are eaten on this day. The cakes are shaped after the triangular *taschen* (pockets) of the tyrant, Haman, whose downfall was brought about by the brave Queen Esther, and so are called *Hamantaschen,* or "Haman's pockets." Despite the use of the German-derived word for pockets, some say that the three-sided pastries resemble the purse that Haman carried. Others have said that they are fashioned after the tricorne hat he usually wore.

During their centuries of persecution, the Jews encountered many Hamans and frequently celebrated local Purims of victory over thwarted oppressors. The arriving Jews of turn-of-the-century New York City came up against a Haman of their own in the person of the city's immigration commissioner, who illegally imposed his own condition for entry into the United States. He decreed that no immigrant who did not have twenty-five dollars on his person could pass through Ellis Island.

As this was a great deal of money at the time, especially for the fleeing poor, and as very few knew of this stipulation when they left Europe, thousands arrived in New York harbor only to be rejected and sent back. A fierce outcry on the part of Jewish immigrant organizations and newspapers at last alerted the federal authorities to this injustice, and not long afterward the "Haman of Ellis Island," as he had become known, resigned. Once more, a suitable occasion had arisen for the baking and eating of Hamantaschen, for, on the whole, New York City had proved itself to be a Jewish haven.

In general, however, there was a rapidly growing trend toward the restriction of immigration. After 1900, local massacres and increasing revolutionary activity in Russia continued to send waves of Jewish immigrants to the United States. By 1914, two million had arrived. But now, the "open door" was slowly beginning to close, not only for the Jews but for all ethnic groups.

The 1920s saw the enactment of both "quota" and "national origin" laws. These were designed not only to reduce immigration but to prevent major changes in the ethnic composition of the United States as it existed at the time. The nineteenth-century pioneers of the cities had made their contribution and now they saw their day dissolve. Like the pioneers of the wilderness, during that same era, they had met and conquered America's last frontier.

Recipes from

---

the Pioneers
of the Cities

⁊ *POTS DE CRÈME*

    2   cups light cream (1 pint), or 1 cup milk and 1
        cup heavy cream
    6   egg yolks
    8   tablespoons sugar
        pinch salt
 1 ½ teaspoons vanilla extract

Preheat oven to 325 degrees Fahrenheit. Pour 1¾
cups of the cream into a saucepan and heat, on moderately high heat, until tiny bubbles appear around rim
and a skin forms on top of cream. Meanwhile, place egg
yolks in a medium-size mixing bowl and beat with a wire
whisk until slightly thickened and paler in color. Beat in
the sugar, a few tablespoons at a time, the salt, the vanilla, and remaining ¼ cup of cold cream.

Pour the hot cream through a strainer to remove skin.
Add cream, a little at a time, to egg mixture, beating
well with wire whisk. Pour mixture into six small ce-
ramic baking pots (4-ounce size) or six heatproof glass
custard cups. Arrange cream pots or glass cups in a
large baking pan and add water to baking pan to a
depth of about one inch.

Bake for 45 minutes or until a sharp knife inserted into centers comes out clean. Cool and chill. Serve directly from cream pots. Or, to remove *pots de crème* from glass cups, run a sharp knife all around edge, invert over a small dessert dish, and tap to loosen. Although very rich, this dessert is delicious topped with brandied cherries or apricots, or with raspberry or strawberry sauce and/or a small dab of whipped cream. Serves 6.

⋖§ SENATE BEAN SOUP

1	cup white pea beans
4	cups boiling water
	ham bone with meat on it, or thick piece of ham (¼ to ½ pound meat)
1	tablespoon butter
1	medium-size onion, diced very fine
1½	teaspoons salt
¼	teaspoon white pepper

Measure beans into a strainer or sieve and rinse well under cold water. Place in a bowl, add water to cover, and let beans soak overnight.

Next day drain off water. Bring the 4 cups of water to a boil in a large soup pot. Add beans and ham bone or ham. Cover pot and simmer one hour.

Meanwhile melt the butter in a small frying pan, add onion and sauté just until golden. Add to soup, which has cooked one hour, and simmer one-half hour more. Remove ham bone or ham piece. Remove half the beans and half the soup liquid and put them through a coarse sieve. Return mixture to soup pot along with any of the beans that have not been mashed through the sieve. Cut ham into small pieces, removing bone and fat, and return to soup.

Add salt and pepper, adjusting seasoning to taste. Reheat and serve. Makes 6 servings. (This recipe is adapted from that of the United States Senate Restaurant.)

⇜ *IRISH SODA BREAD*

2	cups sifted all-purpose flour
2	tablespoons sugar
1	teaspoon salt
½	teaspoon baking soda
½	teaspoon cream of tartar
½	cup butter or margarine (¼ pound or 1 stick)
½	cup raisins
1	tablespoon caraway seeds
⅔	cup buttermilk or sour milk*
1	egg, slightly beaten

Set oven to heat to 375 degrees Fahrenheit. Combine flour, sugar, salt, baking soda, and cream of tartar, and sift into a medium-large mixing bowl. Cut butter or margarine into chunks, add to dry mixture and with a pastry blender or two knives, cut in shortening to the size of peas. Add raisins and caraway seeds. Add milk and egg all at once and stir mixture with a fork just until blended.

Turn mixture into a greased 9-inch pie plate, keeping it away from edges of plate and mounding it in center. With a sharp knife, mark four slashes on top in the shape of a cross. Bake about 30 minutes or until soda bread is browned on top and has a hollow sound when thumped. (Surface may be slightly cracked in places.)

*To make sour milk, add 2 teaspoons white vinegar to ⅔ cup fresh sweet milk and let stand a few seconds until clabbered.

Serve warm or cool, cut into cakelike wedges, with butter and jam if desired. Makes about 10 slices.

◄§ *HAMANTASCHEN*

½   cup butter (¼ pound or 1 stick), softened at
      room temperature
¼   cup solid vegetable shortening, at room temper-
      ature
⅓   cup sugar
 1   egg
 1   teaspoon vanilla extract
 2   cups sifted all-purpose flour
½   teaspoon salt
*Prune Butter Filling**
½   pound prunes
½   cup sugar
 1   teaspoon lemon juice
¼   teaspoon cinnamon

To prepare filling, soak prunes overnight in water. Next day pit prunes, place in saucepan, add water just to cover, and sugar. Cover pan and simmer about one hour or until mixture is thick. Add lemon juice and cinnamon. Check flavor, adding more sugar if necessary. Cool thoroughly before using.

To prepare pastry, preheat oven to 350 degrees Fahrenheit. Combine butter and vegetable shortening in a large mixing bowl, and cream with back of a wooden spoon until smooth and well blended. Add sugar and continue creaming until fluffy. Add egg and vanilla and

---

*If available, commercially prepared prune butter, also known as *lekvar,* can be used. For this recipe, about 1½ cups are needed.

beat well. Add mixture of flour and salt, a little at a time, blending in well with wooden spoon. Gather dough together, wrap in wax paper, and chill for about one-half hour.

Divide chilled dough in half. Roll out first half (keeping rest refrigerated) with a floured rolling pin, on a floured pastry cloth or board, to a 9 × 12 rectangle, about ⅛-inch thick. Cut into twelve 3-inch squares. Place a generous teaspoon of prune butter in center of each. To form *Hamantaschen,* bring two adjoining corners to the center atop filling. Seal their adjoining sides together by pinching dough into a ridge. Now bring up remaining side and pinch each end to corner of dough directly opposite. Center should be left open, showing some of filling. The sides of the triangle will not be equal in length.

Place Hamantaschen on a lightly greased cookie sheet, not too close together, and bake at 350 degrees for 20 to 25 minutes, or until lightly browned. Remove and cool on wire rack. Repeat with second half of dough. Makes 24 Hamantaschen.

On the Eve
of the Twentieth Century

"I MAGINE . . ." A TRAVEL-
weary Mark Twain wrote from Europe near the turn
of the century, "a mighty porterhouse steak an inch
and a half thick, hot and sputtering from the griddle;
dusted with fragrant pepper; enriched with little melting bits of butter . . . and imagine . . . a great cup of
American home-made coffee, with the cream a-froth on
top, some real butter, firm and yellow and fresh, some
smoking-hot biscuits, a plate of hot buckwheat cakes,
with transparent syrup. . . ."

The meal the homesick American writer was describ-
ing in his book, *A Tramp Abroad,* was the typical American breakfast of the 1890s. The country had, of course,
long since arrived at the age of overeating. There was
usually meat for breakfast—beefsteak, mutton chops,
veal cutlet, ham, or sausages—as well as eggs and potatoes, hotcakes and porridge, quickbreads and coffee.
Coffee had become the all-American washing-down beverage, usually taken with plenty of cream and sugar and
drunk not only after but during meals, almost as wine
and beer were drunk in Europe.

Dinner, the main meal of the day, was traditionally
served in the early afternoon on the farm, but among

those who lived in the cities it gradually developed into an evening meal. However, it lost none of its extravagances: its fried, roasted, and gravied meats and game; its starchy overcooked vegetables and soggy greens; its lard-rich pies, dumplings, cobblers, and heavy, sweet bread puddings.

Nor were the lunches that city people ate away from home skimpy affairs, for oyster parlors, chophouses, and hotel dining rooms offered ample and filling midday fare. Besides, there was always the "free lunch," an institution that came about as a result of the rivalry between neighborhood saloons and that reached its peak in New York and other cities in the late 1800s and early 1900s.

For the price of a couple of five-cent beers or ten-cent shots of whiskey, a customer was entitled to help himself from the free-lunch counter with its array of hot and cold foods such as ham, roast beef, sausages, pickles, herrings, cheese, hard-boiled eggs, potato salad, pork and beans, and occasionally even hot soups and stews. Most of these dishes, of course, were highly seasoned on the theory that the customer's thirst would spur the purchase of additional drinks.

The "free lunch" was yet another indication of America's food abundance and of the way so many Americans were overindulging their appetites by the turn of the century. It was not surprising that the term, "American plan," was adopted to indicate a hotel guest rate that included three hearty daily meals in the price of the room. President McKinley ran successfully for reelection in 1900 on the campaign slogan: "Four more years of the full dinner pail," for the well-rounded paunch was one of the principal symbols of American prosperity.

There were, however, Americans who deplored the

gluttony and the unmannerly eating habits of so many of their countrymen. Those critics also sensed, long before the days of nutrition study, that most meals were badly balanced, leaning too heavily toward meats, fats, starches, and sugars. Dyspepsia was a common complaint. As early as the 1830s, a temperance movement advocating moderation in both eating and drinking had begun to take form. A New Jersey minister named Sylvester Graham advised the use of breads and cereals made with whole wheat flour, rather than refined white flour, along with a vegetarian diet, thorough chewing, and meals eaten in an atmosphere of relaxed cheerfulness rather than rude haste.

Graham also believed that a meatless diet of whole grains, milk, and fresh fruits and vegetables would reduce the desire for alcohol. Grahamite societies and boarding houses sprang up in his name, as did graham flour and graham bread. But the relatively small number of his followers were considered food faddists for, when it came to the dinner table, the tendency of the day was to more than make up for the austerity of the colonial past.

Dietary changes were, nevertheless, on the way. In 1876, Dr. John Kellogg of Battle Creek, Michigan, developed a precooked dried wheat preparation to serve to his patients at the vegetarian health institute where he presided. Although intended as a between-meals health snack, Kellogg's creation was soon adopted as a breakfast food, eaten with milk and sugar on it. Shortly afterward, his brother Will developed cornflakes; a Colorado man brought forth Shredded Wheat; and Charles W. Post arrived on the scene with Grape Nuts and Postum (a coffee substitute made with grains). The rest is familiar history.

The turn of the century saw the lightening of the formerly groaning American breakfast table, as office workers and others in sedentary jobs began to turn from the heavy and time-consuming cooked breakfast to the quick convenience of packaged dry cereal. The addition of orange juice and grapefruit to the morning repast did not come until after the discovery of Vitamin C in 1913.

While convenience foods were still far too few to take the family cook out of the kitchen, aids such as canned foods and refrigeration did come on the scene. The first factory-canned tomatoes and canned pork-and-beans appeared shortly before the Civil War. Techniques of preservation advanced so rapidly that, in the closing decades of the 1800s, perishables like sardines, salmon, and milk in safe, long-keeping tins began to appear on grocery shelves.

The railroads pioneered the first refrigerator cars as early as the 1840s and set the pattern for the home iceboxes of the post-Civil War era. At the same time, refrigerated railroad cars were able to swiftly transport fresh milk, fruits, vegetables, and meats from distant sources, improving diets and lessening the average family's dependence on root vegetables and salt-cured meats.

If the cook did not yet manage to escape the kitchen during the closing decades of the nineteenth century, at least the rest of the family did. The cast-iron cookstove began to take the place of the kitchen fireplace, and heating stoves were installed in parlors, dining rooms, dens, and occasionally even in bedrooms. The women with their knitting and sewing, the men with their cigars and newspapers, and the children with their lessons and games moved into other areas of the house, leaving the onetime family-gathering room to specialize in kitchen functions only.

There was no question that the average American diet, with all its imperfections, was raising taller and huskier individuals in 1900 than in 1800. By the 1880s, manufacturers of ready-to-wear clothing were revising their scale of sizes—upward! A less promising development, however, was the immense gap that was opening between the diets of the rich and the poor, not only in terms of quantity and variety, but in terms of food quality.

These differences were far less evident in the farming countryside than in the cities, where the immigrant families tended to live as frugally as possible on staples of bread and tea. Among the other foods on which the city poor spent their hard-earned incomes, the milk that was sold to them was usually diluted with water, the butter adulterated with hog fat, and the meat, fowl, and fish tainted with disease or decay. Children were enticed to buy penny candies that were brightly colored with toxic substances, and the many homeless and indigent ate miserable ashcan scraps in advanced states of putrefaction. Pure food laws were still a long way off, and those that had been enacted were seldom enforced. The inspectors were bought off by the entrepreneurs, and the health and welfare of the nation's poor were sacrificed to their greed.

At the same time, among the prosperous, the "Gilded Age" flowed on. Mark Twain had coined this term to describe the final decades of the nineteenth century, also known as the "Gay Nineties," the "Gaslight Era," and the "Gingerbread Age" (because of its taste for showy decoration). But Mark Twain said it best, for the word "gilded" rather than "golden" expressed how superficial, how merely skin-deep was this era of national wealth and well-being.

The average worker of the 1890s labored sixty hours

a week for a wage of twelve dollars. Depressions were frequent, and social benefits did not exist. The country's many multimillionaires, on the other hand, paid no taxes. Perhaps the greatest flaunting of the personal wealth of this period was a costume ball given in 1897 at New York's Waldorf-Astoria Hotel by one of the city's super-rich citizens. The hotel ballroom was decorated to resemble a hall at the Palace of Versailles, with rare tapestries and crystal chandeliers, and the guests arrived in costly replicas of the jeweled costumes worn at the court of Louis XV. One guest wore a suit of gold-inlaid armor valued at $10,000, and the entire affair, including the most sumptuous food and drink that money could buy, was reputed to have cost $369,000!

Americans had indeed come a long way in the century since the post-Revolutionary period. The desire for change and betterment of the pioneers of the 1800s had brought about the taming of the wilderness and the building of the cities. The dedication to hard work and the pursuit of economic gain had ushered in an elevated standard of material comforts. Although we think of them today as exaggerated and tasteless, the high-water marks of the good life, in 1900, consisted of overfeeding one's stomach, as well as overdressing one's body and overheating one's home. These evidences of a prosperous nation were enjoyed by the rich and looked to with longing by those on the lower rungs of the economic ladder.

In the century that was to follow, new social patterns would emerge. America's eating habits would be buffeted about by a series of changes based on the study of nutrition, the rapid development of food technology, the proliferation of cookbooks and cooking schools, by foreign dining experiences, fast food franchisers, and many other scientific, cultural, and economic factors.

But the pioneer era, the century of bold expansion and determined settlement, had left its indelible stamp on the national character and on American culture. In spirit, Americans would continue to be ready and willing to move about the country, changing their jobs and relocating their families, and to be socially mobile as well, crossing class barriers with comparative ease. The twentieth-century American would continue to believe in the positive value of hard work, to be creative and resourceful, often a jack-of-all-trades and a do-it-yourselfer, to express optimism and even to indulge in boastfulness.

The growth of the country by regions—separate and distinct geographical and cultural areas—would also continue to contribute rich and diverse flavors. These would show up in the various styles of housing, clothing, work and recreation patterns, and of course in cuisine. Even though today's chili parlors in Chicago and frozen pecan pies in New England supermarkets seem to defy and dilute the regional heritage of pioneer America, the characteristic dishes are still to be found in their places of origin. Often, today, a burgoo or gumbo, a Swedish coffeecake or an Irish tea scone, a Cornish pasty or a Portuguese fish stew, made from a treasured recipe handed down by a settler ancestor, appears on a family table.

Whatever cooking trends and culinary fads and fashions the twentieth century would bring—and they would be many—the long, formative pioneer period would continue to wield its influence on American life.

✒ AN AFTERWORD ABOUT MEASUREMENTS

THOMAS JEFFERSON GREATLY ADMIRED French culture and learning. He had high praise for the metric system, a standard of measurements developed in France. Based on a decimal scale, "metric" was a convenient way of expressing weight, volume, distance, and other measurements in units known as grams, liters, and meters.

As early as 1790, Jefferson advocated the use of the metric system in the United States. But the English system with its ounces and pounds, its cups, pints, quarts, and gallons, its inches, feet, and miles had already become entrenched in colonial and post-colonial America.

Although the Congress ruled the metric system legal in 1866, pioneer America stayed with the clumsy but familiar English system. Today, however, "metric" is on the march in the everyday life of the United States. Many schools teach it, many communities have adopted it, and many packaged food products show the weight or volume of their contents in metric as well as English units.

The amounts of the ingredients called for in the recipes in this book can be converted to metric units as follows:

WEIGHT			VOLUME		
1 ounce	=	28 grams	1 teaspoon	=	5 milliliters
3½ ounces	=	100 grams	1 tablespoon	=	15 milliliters
4 ounces	=	114 grams	1 fluid ounce	=	30 milliliters
8 ounces	=	227 grams	1 cup	=	0.24 liters
1 pound	=	0.45 kilograms	1 pint	=	0.47 liters
2.2 pounds	=	1 kilogram	1 quart	=	0.95 liters

(to convert grams to ounces, multiply by .035)

(to convert liters to quarts, multiply by 1.06)

Index